SHADOWS
of the
NIGHT

How One Man Survived the Trauma of Adoption,
the Snares of the Music Business,
and Found His Birthmother and Seven Sisters

D.L. BYRON

Printed in the United States of America.

Cover Art Watercolor: Mimi
Cover Design: JuLee Brand for Kevin Anderson & Associates
Author Photo: Desmond Byron

Shadows of the Night/ D.L. Byron. —1st ed.

Hardcover ISBN 978-1-7335650-2-8

Paperback ISBN 978-1-7335650-0-4

eBook 978-1-7335650-1-1

Contents

SPECIAL THANKS

A special thanks to all of my family, without whose love and support this work would not have been possible.

1966

I was fifteen years old and she had blacked out once again. One second she was standing there, nodding her head to one of my adolescent stories about school, and the next she was on the floor stretched out in a rag doll sprawl.

Panic only mildly set in this time. My heart was still beating normally as I pondered what to do with her frail body. I couldn't drag her through the living room because I might mess up the perfectly vacuumed, never disturbed or stepped-on blue, plush carpet. Those perfectly straight lines left behind by the vacuum would be gone. There would be hell to pay if I did that.

She stirred, coming to long enough to ask me for water. Within seconds I was at the tap, filling up a glass. I turned back around and looked down at her limp form. She was out again. Now the panic started to set in. This episode seemed more serious than any before. I could hear my heart beating louder than the radio on the kitchen counter. What's more, I could feel it. I struggled to breathe. I realized that I had to do something, and fast, or the shell of a woman that I called my mother might soon be dead.

Get her off the floor. She weighed all of 125 pounds, if she was lucky. When she wasn't on the floor completely unconscious she stood 5'4". I could pick her up. All I had to do was throw her over my shoulder and keep her head from hitting the wall. The floral apron haphazardly tied around her waist seemed out of place now. It was the kind of apron that belonged on the ideal TV mom from the fifties, not on my addled and moribund mother. But there it was, lying almost perfectly across her legs, a crumpled pack of Chesterfields peeking out of one of the pockets.

I knelt down in front of her, wrapped my arms around her, and attempted to sit her up. She was dead weight. There would be no superhero-carrying-over-the-shoulder for me. I moved behind her instead, and cupped my hands under her armpits. I'd have to drag her after all, which meant I had no choice but to disturb the perfectly vacuumed lines on the blue plush carpet. She came to again, struggling to form words. "The guest room," she managed.

The guest room? Why the guest room? Why not her own bedroom? Hunched over and still struggling to breathe, I continued to drag her down the hall and around the corner. I hoisted her onto the bed, slipped her shoes off, and covered her with the soft, yellow blanket she kept folded there.

"Get me a cup of tea," she whispered.

I don't think I had ever, in my short, adolescent life, seen that woman drink tea. Coffee? Always. Tea? Never. This seemingly insignificant detail completely threw me off. I became scared and confused. We only keep tea in the house for guests.

I went back to the kitchen. My heart was palpitating normally now and my breathing had slowed down. I stared blankly at the cup I had prepared. I could hear the radio again.

"A Whiter Shade of Pale" eerily wafted through the kitchen. That song, how ironic, I thought, given her pallor.

When I returned to the guest room, my mother had fallen asleep. Putting the tea down on the night table, I nudged her gently. Her eyes flew open and she looked at me without recognition. Within seconds, fear took hold and she started screaming at me like I was an intruder. She pulled the yellow blanket to the chin of her pale face, crying like a child, "No! No! Ahhhhh!" like I was the boogeyman.

Backing away from the bed, I put my hands in front of me to show her I meant no harm. "Hey, it's me, Mom . . . It's me, it's me!" I said over and over again as she kept screaming and shrieking unintelligible things at the top of her lungs. And then, she blinked twice, went silent, and her face changed. She recognized me now. The screaming stopped and the agony was over, for now.

It was moments like these when I would reflect on the reality that only my adoptive mother would carry on like this. My real mother would never act this way. Mostly, because she was perfect. My real mother was out there, somewhere, and one day she would find me. One day, she would come for me, rescue me. She would show me the kind of love that I would see on *The Brady Bunch*. She would tell me how sorry she was for giving me up and wave a magic wand so all of my pain and sorrow would fade away. Inevitably, she would be my savior and cast out these demons, these shadows of the night.

CHAPTER 1

BREATHE

My mother drove the Mercury like a madwoman, veering the turns with wide eyes, gripping the steering wheel with a kitchen knife in one hand, and a burning cigarette in the other. I couldn't breathe. As she whipped around corners to get me to the hospital, I bounced around the front seat like a pinball gasping for air. I wound up in a twisted position so as to give me a view of the clear blue sky through the windshield. I could see the telephone poles whizzing by, all the while wondering if we would end up on the side of the road so she could perform an emergency tracheotomy on me. She had long since explained in "child's terms" just what that procedure was. My mother was a registered nurse, so I knew she could do it. She would whip that big red Mercury over to the roadside, push me down flat on the red and white vinyl seats, and save my alarmed little life by sinking a razor-sharp kitchen knife into my throat. At the tender age of five, that image scared the living shit out of me.

The emergency tracheotomy never happened, but the bouts of me not being able to breathe continued. I had asthma and allergies, so difficulty breathing was the norm. Very few doctors prescribed rescue inhalers in those days, so kids like me were forced to stick it out trying not to panic.

I think my mom thought she got a dud of a kid when she adopted me. The fact that both my parents smoked cigarettes incessantly hardly crossed their minds as they tried to understand why I couldn't breathe normally. But dud or not, I was theirs, and had been since I was just a few weeks old.

I was given up for adoption shortly after I was born. According to my Record of Birth, I was born on December 18th, 1952, in Trenton, New Jersey. Unlike a birth certificate, a Record of Birth is a legal document on which the state records a birth that occurs out of wedlock. But none of that seemed to matter to my adoptive parents, Ann and Joseph Mesiano. They just wanted a baby. For all intents and purposes, they were a seemingly normal couple living in the town of Vineland, New Jersey, that simply couldn't conceive. This was a tough realization for my mother, especially because all of her friends and neighbors were bearing children or adopting. Why not the Mesianos? So my parents, not wanting to be left out in the "barren" cold, turned to the Catholic Church for help.

The Archdiocese of Camden came through. My parents were successful in acquiring a boy child who would have wavy red hair and a big round face. They named that child Gary David Mesiano. They couldn't have picked a more contrasting baby. My mom was of Ukrainian descent, she had blonde wavy hair and sharp facial features. My father, Sicilian, had very dark hair and olive skin. My brand-new parents wanted a regular kid who would go to school, engage in sports, get married, have children, and maybe buy a house with a white picket fence. What they wanted was a normal kid with a normal life. What they got was anything but.

I could sense things. For example, I could sense that somehow I didn't belong to these people I called my parents. Even at the age of five, I had silent inexpressible concerns. Something felt off. It didn't really seem to me that they were all that happy with each other. But those sensations were nothing compared to the supernatural oddities that I began to experience. We lived in a small two bedroom redbrick house on the corner of Main Road and Roberts Boulevard in Vineland. From the outside it sat, unassuming, like any other house on the block. But inside, something strange was waiting. There were many nights I would fall quietly asleep, only to be woken up in the wee hours gasping desperately for air. It felt like someone was sitting on my chest, crushing me so I couldn't breathe. Invisible hands covered my mouth so I couldn't scream. My eyes searched wildly in the dark for what was suffocating me, but I always came up empty. I never saw a thing.

I recall another time when my little mind homed in on something out of the ordinary. I was in the living room, sitting on the floor playing with my Tinkertoys, when I thought I heard my mother calling me from the basement. I got up and went toward the basement door and I stopped and watched as the door slowly opened by itself. I heard her voice again. Sure that she was downstairs I toddled over to the open doorway to find her, looking down into the cellar. I wound up falling down the wooden steps, hurting my head. My mother, who was outside hanging laundry and nowhere near the basement, was hysterical when she found me. I think she thought the adoption agency was going to come and take me away, citing her as an unfit mother. But that didn't happen.

As strange as those instances were, I think the most disturbing paranormal event happened the day I felt some kind of strange magnetic force coming from my parents' bedroom. I walked by the room when I felt myself being drawn inside. So in I went, slowly, cautiously, looking carefully around as I entered. Nothing. I sat on the bed. Still nothing. Then, without a warning, the closet door opened ever so slowly and what looked like a bony hand appeared, beckoning to me with its index finger. I sat there frozen with fear. I wanted to run, but I couldn't. It was like something was holding me there. But in a sudden moment's release, after what seemed like an eternity, I was able to get up and dart out of the room as if I was on fire.

I didn't share these ghostly encounters with my mother. I didn't have to. I was certain she sensed something too. Within what seemed like only a month, we were moving out of the house on Main and Roberts and into a rented house on Arcadia Place. As we packed boxes in one house and unpacked them again in another, a brand-new house was being built for us in a developing neighborhood about a mile away on Holmes Avenue. It was far from ready, but there it was, growing walls and floors, one day at a time. As we settled into the rental on Arcadia, I asked my mother why we moved. I waited for her to tell me about her own experiences with the bony hand or the lady in the basement. But she didn't. Instead, she delivered an answer that puzzled me.

"We moved because you're allergic to bricks," she said.

I suspected that I might be allergic to lots of things, but bricks? I thought her response was odd. Could it be that she had her own experiences in the house but had no idea how to process them? Or was this the harbinger of an all too common behavior of my mother laying blame and attempting to make me the scapegoat? It would become her way of explaining everything that went wrong in our family. After all, because of my asthma, my mother had reluctantly given up her prized long-haired red Persian cat "Rusty." I don't think she ever forgave me for that.

That small area of South Jersey had become the poultry capital of the US at the time. The land was flat, perfect for farming or putting up chicken coops. Poultry was big business. My father was a salesman for Rudco, a local company that made chicken feeders and other products that served the industry. Sometimes I would go with my father on a weekend to service some farmer's feeder. My dad was pretty handy with things like that. He never really talked too much and those "fix it" trips were the only times that he and I spent alone together. One Sunday afternoon we drove to a farm way out on the other side of town, driving for miles along lonely roads that cracked through green fields. When my father had finished the job we drove over to the main house to get his pay. Out came the owner with some cash and a live chicken that he held by its neck. My father thanked the man, took the cash, and tossed the chicken in the back of the station wagon. I had noticed that the farmer had numbers tattooed on his arm and as we drove away I asked, "Dad, why did that man have numbers on him?"

"Something that happened during the war." He snorted, not wanting to discuss it.

I later found out that my father had served in the Army during World War II, he made the rank of Sergeant and was involved in liberating one of the concentration camps. Eventually I would find out even more about him. He was one of thirteen children. Apparently his father was a tyrant and kicked Joseph out of his house after catching him smoking a cigarette in a chicken coop. Smoking in coops was strictly forbidden given the sawdust and wood chips that were used to cover the cement floor. Eventually, he and his father reconciled. Years later, as a young man, my father purchased a decent car and a small plot of land that he had left in the care of his father when he shipped off to Germany. I suppose that since he and his father had resolved their differences, Joe felt confident that his father would look after those things. My father returned from the war somewhat shell-shocked, only to discover that his own father had sold everything off and pocketed the money. Maybe that's why when he wasn't occasionally exaggerating to make himself appear important, he hardly ever said a word unless spoken to. He was normally almost absent. Later that day my father took the chicken into the garage and slit its neck. He had already moved the cars into the driveway in anticipation of the butchery. I swear that the chicken was still screaming as the blood spurted from its body. It's really true what they say about chickens running around with their heads cut off. There was blood all over the garage and my father's work pants.

Most kids start kindergarten at age five. Not me. I was tossed directly into the first grade with a goodly number of very angry, frustrated nuns who didn't like little boys very much and practiced corporal punishment as often as they said the rosary. Maybe my mother thought that it was me who needed to be "exorcised" and that's why she sent me to Sacred Heart Parochial School, to be cleansed of my five-year-old sins. That first day of school is still alive in my mind. Everyone in the class had already taken their seat while my mother and I stood in the hallway. She shoved St. Joseph's aspirins down my throat in a futile attempt to calm me down. I was scared and had put up a fuss all morning. I had never really played with any other kids very much so I didn't know what to expect. I just stood there shaking as I looked through the open door at a class full of strangers being led by a woman who was dressed in what appeared to be a Batman costume. As it turned out, my only saving grace was a boy I sat behind in class named Edward Dondero. He began swinging his hand behind him, just over my desk, pretending to dare me to hit it. I pretended to stab at his hand with a pencil. At recess Sister Anna Thomas pulled out a big can of foot-long hard pretzels and sold them for a penny apiece. I wanted one but I was mortified that I didn't have a penny. Ed had two so he gave me one. We became fast friends. In stature we were kinda like Laurel and Hardy. I was thin and he was heavy. We both had a good sense of humor and spent a lot of time together laughing and cracking jokes. By third grade we were going to see science-fiction movies on Saturday afternoons at the local theatre in town. My mom would drop me off at his house around eleven on a Saturday morning and his mother would give us lunch before we walked the short distance into town to the movie theatre. I always devoured my lunch immediately and then would sit with my head in my hands waiting for Ed to magnificently masticate every last morsel of his meal. "This guy's gonna live forever," I thought, "just like one of those giant turtles on TV." He never knew it, but Edward would become a savior in my young life.

As early as third grade, I began to notice that I didn't look anything like my parents. When I asked my mother why, she told me that I was adopted, and therefore, "I was special." Now I understood why I never felt like I belonged to these people. It was because they really weren't my people. They weren't my real parents. They weren't the mom and dad that smiled proudly through the glass window of the nursery the day I was born, as I lay wrapped in a blanket next to half a dozen other babies in the hospital. No. And according to my adoptive mother, my real mother had died in childbirth.

I can clearly remember the impact that statement had on me and my eight year old brain. The fact that she died in childbirth immediately told me that I was somehow responsible for her death. I alone was the reason she flatlined on the table. That fact churned my insides out and took my breath away. I had killed someone without even knowing how to kill. I swallowed that pill whole and held it down, never discussing it with anyone. I was a killer.

I didn't want to believe what my mother was telling me. The part of me that didn't want to believe her was that same part that would fantasize about the day my real parents would come for me. They would thank my adoptive parents for taking care of me, and then sweep me away to their lavish home with an ornate winding staircase and fancy cars in the drive. No ghosts, no blaming, and no blood on my hands. I would fit right in and all would be right in my world.

While I was busy daydreaming about being spirited away to my invisible parents' palace, my mother was beginning to exhibit strange behaviors that I really didn't understand. She started talking to herself which wasn't so strange at first but soon she began to answer herself as well. Almost always speaking in a frantic voice she became two people. If I happened to walk up behind her while she was talking she would scream at me wildly for frightening her. She seemed to be irrational for most of the day but this behavior would completely vanish when my father got home from work. I had no idea at the time what actually caused this erratic demeanor. All I knew was that she smoked two packs of cigarettes a day and drank coffee incessantly. Could it be that the combination of these things actually made my mother so unpredictable? For a kid, not knowing who or what to expect every time I turned around made existing in my house tenuous. I became withdrawn and was given to hiding away in my room. The woman who was so willing to save my alarmed little life just a few short years ago now seemed agitated at my very presence.

She had moved on from her career as a nurse, after leaving a job at the New Jersey State School which housed and treated kids with Down syndrome. Part of her job was to bathe the patients. I think the final straw broke when one too many of the patients pooped in the tub. She decided to pursue her talents as a seamstress. Setting up shop in the basement of our new home on Holmes Avenue, my mother worked late at night using two sewing machines, one called a "blind stitcher." My father made a makeshift table of plywood set over two wooden horses for her to lay out her material. She stitched together drapes of all kinds, her specialty was ceiling to floor, filling orders from the Mill End Center, the only fabric store in town. From the bed in my dark room, I could hear the buzzing of her machines coming from the basement below me. The rhythmic sounds sometimes lulled me to a certain sleep, where I would dream lofty dreams of becoming somebody. I didn't realize it at the time, but being adopted into this family began to cast a dark shadow over me. I felt untethered, there was no grounding, no love. I didn't belong here and no one appreciated me. If anything, I felt like I was in the way of this frantic sewing machine that I called my mother. And my father? He never said very much.

The air was heavy in our house. Ed was the only one brave enough to come over, and I was always happy when he did. His presence was a relief from the tension that I lived with day to day. I knew he felt uncomfortable at times, but he was brave enough to dismiss it and more than happy to be my distraction. He was the only person that I could actually confide in. Despite my trust in him, I never openly discussed what it felt like to live in that house. I didn't have to. Ed knew me better than anyone else ever would. He was my first and best friend. Most other friends would only dare occasionally show their faces.

My mother wanted others to believe that we had much more money than we actually did. She took most of the money that she made from making drapes and bought all new Italian Provincial furniture for the living and dining room. We had a sunken living room, which she had carpeted with a very high royal blue plush. No one was allowed to use the living room because our body weight would leave footprints on the carpet. She did the same with the dining room but had a clear plastic runner going from the kitchen to the family room so no one would dare step on the rug. I wondered what my father actually thought about all this and why he simply just went along with it. The family room was the only place that anyone could sit. She had even gone as far as to put a TV in my bedroom, but wouldn't allow me to connect it or even be in my room with the door closed. She just wanted people to see that I was fortunate enough to have a TV in my room. There was also a bathroom right next to my bedroom but I could only use the toilet and the sink. My mother had hung velvet drapes over the tub that were drawn open by velvet straps with tassels on the ends. We all used the tiny shower that was between my parents' bedroom and the laundry room.

Most of our relatives simply stayed at bay. With the exception of a few aunts and uncles, our kitchen table rarely saw guests. Sometimes my father's family would come over with my cousins, who were always a breath of fresh air. We were always happy to see each other, and I would have fun entertaining them. All my Italian cousins, Delores, Maria, Mary, Eleanore and the rest, they all knew well enough not to touch anything. Absolutely everyone felt the fear of being banished from a house that was slowly becoming a museum.

Once in a while my mother's brother, John, would visit with his wife, Olga, and their son Paul. Those visits stopped after Olga passed away. Uncle John stopped drinking, smoking, and cursing and joined the local Assembly of God, a place of worship that some referred to as the "Holy Roller" church, a brand of Christianity that today would be called "Evangelical." The church paired him up with a new wife, Helen, who gave birth to two more children. Then Uncle John died of a massive heart attack. Helen had asked him to fix a kitchen cabinet the day after his release from the hospital, already having suffered a very close call. My mom never forgave Helen for that and I don't think she liked us very much either. She believed we had the devil in us. No one was comfortable around my mother anyway, except for my Aunt Marie, my mother's half sister.

Ah, Aunt Marie, I just loved that woman. She was a fun, jovial lady with a rapier wit and a giant beehive hairdo that somehow miraculously fit into her cool little Mercury Comet compact car. She and my Uncle Tony were my two favorite people. They understood me, especially Aunt Marie. I felt love from them. We visited them at their big old farmhouse just outside of town. They had a real pear tree in their backyard that was often surrounded by swarms of yellow jackets in the summer if the fruit was left to overripen. Despite being allergic to almost everything, I wasn't allergic to bees. I wasn't afraid of them, either. So I volunteered to pick the pears. When I came back inside with a basket full, Aunt Marie gave me club soda to drink. Drinking that clear bubbly made me feel so sophisticated.

When I wasn't at Aunt Marie's, she was at our house, working her magic to try and get my mother to loosen up. She knew how my mother could be toward me, and always came to my rescue. She often did this when I brought home a bad report card. Aunt Marie was a well needed respite from my mother's grip. She appreciated me for who I was and knew that I was both smart and talented. What she didn't know was that I was dyslexic.

No one knew. I don't recall when dyslexia or ADHD were actually discovered or qualified as a diagnosis. In those days, it just didn't exist. If you got bad grades because you unwittingly saw numbers and words backwards or reversed, you were considered a poor student or just plain stupid. Unfortunately that was me, and as a result, I struggled academically. I wasn't great at math, which in turn would mean that I wouldn't be great at reading music either. But I had an ear for music, and to me that was all that mattered. Fine art and poetry would find their way into my world later. It was during these first years in Catholic school that I became interested in music. It offered me an escape from what was happening in our house. I was enthralled by whatever was on the radio and even TV, except for Lawrence Welk. It was clear that I was one of those creative types because I had already developed a talent for drawing and daydreaming. This talent was purely mine. My parents didn't understand it. Music and art were not part of our household, not part of their world. This was mine. It defined me. Music grabbed my attention and just pulled me in. I was captured by the layers that pop stars of the day were weaving together. For me, it had become irresistible. Aunt Marie bought me a little 45 rpm record player for Christmas. Every time my mother had to go into town I would beg her to let me buy just one 45. Pretty soon I had a nice little collection going. These records would take me to another realm away from the static that was my life. I would sit alone in my room listening to the same song over and over, driving my parents crazy. I started to sing a little and dabble with instruments at any opportunity. My parents had few friends but one couple they knew had an organ. When we would visit them I would doodle around with it, imagining myself up on stage wowing the crowds. Slipping inside of a melody made me feel good about myself and offered me the chance to feel the possibility of being admired. I wanted that feeling desperately. Pretty soon I began lobbying my parents to buy me a piano. I had my eye on a new one I had seen in a nearby music store. My mother knew which one I wanted. She struck a deal with me: "Your father and I will buy you that piano if you promise not to go around the neighborhood and tell everyone about it."

So I went right out the back door and told one of the girls next door. How could I not? I was eight years old and I was getting a brand-new piano! Certain my conversation with the little girl next door would remain confidential, I headed home, proud and excited. As I came in the back door, my mother looked at me with her arms crossed over her apron and said, " You're going to have to be happy with a used piano."

"Why?" I asked.

"Because you didn't keep your promise, that's why," she said sharply as she stomped off into the basement to sew her curtains.

How did she know?

In later years I came to realize that she didn't know at all. How could she? She only knew for sure that I couldn't resist telling someone. So to avoid the expense of buying the new piano that she had promised, she decided to pull a fast one. In my home, this is how things typically unfolded. I was set up to fail, time and again at my mother's whim. Her pride was more important than my confidence. When I wasn't being set up, I was being lied to. When I wasn't being lied to, I was being scolded for something that I didn't do. My mother was a maniacal bundle of nerves who seemed to delight at barking at me for no apparent reason. And my father? Still ever silent.

Finally, one Saturday morning my piano arrived. It was an upright. The wood had a light blonde tone to it, but the most interesting thing about it was a mirror placed near to the top of it so I could see my face and another mirror just over the keyboard so I could see my fingers as I played. I began teaching myself how to play by listening to my 45s again and again, and then reproducing what I heard. My mother learned that our next door neighbor had hired a piano teacher for one of the girls. Not to be outdone, she hired the same piano teacher to come to the house on Saturday mornings. He was a quirky older man, who had long unkempt white hair and something of a stale odor. Mr. Thompson played the organ at a church in Millville, the next town over. Quirky as he was, he thought I was some kind of genius. So much so, that my piano lessons quickly turned into writing sessions. He played a chord and I would tell him if I thought it sounded good or not. Then he would play another. And another. If it didn't sound right, I would say, "No. Go higher. Yes! That's the right one." Before I knew it, we were writing a song called "The Bronze Angel." This collaboration was my first real experience writing music. That was all it took. From that moment on, I was fixated.

At the close of each lesson, Mr. Thompson would assign me a piece to practice. Still hiding the fact that I couldn't read music, I would ask him to play the lesson for me before he left. I would watch his hands move across the keys and listen closely, taking in the melody. I would practice what he played all week long. The following week he would show up again and I would play the piece for him, looking at the sheet music as if I were reading it. Of course I wasn't. He didn't realize this, however, because he thought I was the epitome of a perfect child prodigy. Somehow my mother figured it out, so she fired him. In retrospect, I can only guess that she assumed that she was wasting her money, and eliminating his services could save her budget.

Oddly enough, Mr. Thompson showed up again the very next Saturday and as I stood by the piano in the family room peering over at the front door, I watched him get down on one knee and beg my mother to allow him to teach me again. I don't think he was concerned about having lost the extra money. He simply wanted to teach a student that he believed in. My mother was tremendously embarrassed and after a few moments of frantic indecision, declined his appeal. He stood up, thanked her, turned around and left. As she shut the door behind him, she noticed me watching. We never spoke of it.

Nonetheless, I kept playing and experimenting with composing; when I was lost in the music, I could breathe. I never struggled for air. No car had to take me to the hospital, no entity threatened to cut off my air supply.

CHAPTER 2

REDHEADED FRECKLE-FACED BOY

I first saw the Beatles in February of 1964 when they appeared on the Ed Sullivan show. I was eleven years old at the time and completely struck with wonder. These guys were so cool and they were speaking directly to me, or so I thought. My parents, probably like most other parents of that day, were scared to death. Our family room was filled with my bubbling delight and my parents' abject horror. I remember glancing over at them both sitting on the couch with their eyes pinned wide open and their mouths making the shape of the letter "O." The very next day my father took me to the barbershop to get my first crew cut. I remember him referring to them as "billy goats" as he laughed off his fears with Anthony, the local barber. Of course, Beatlemania had already struck and there was no turning back. The "Mop Tops" were everywhere. As for me, I had just discovered the guitar. Now this was an instrument that I could carry with me, unlike a piano, and impress girls. If I could only learn how to play. My Saturday afternoons with Ed and other friends now included a pilgrimage to the Music Inn on Landis Avenue, our local music shop. I showed up every Saturday afternoon looking for any new or interesting guitars that had just arrived. The clerks in the store would call me out saying, "Here comes Mesiano again to mess up the place." I began saving my allowance and begging my parents for money so I could buy one. Finally, they broke down and with Aunt Marie pitching in I had enough money to buy a well-used Silvertone single cutaway, semi-hollow body, red electric guitar from the Music Inn. In actuality, it was a "jazz" guitar but I didn't care. It was my red electric guitar. My ticket to fame! It cost $65. A lot of money back then.

When I got it home I immediately began to teach myself how to play. I could pretty much just dive in because, as I said, this guitar was a semi-hollow body, which made it audible even without an amplifier. The amp would have to wait. In those days, sheet music came with small guitar graphs above the bars of written music. These diagrams showed you where to position your fingers to make chords. This was a visual way to learn that would totally work for me and my dyslexia. What genius! Pretty soon I became proficient at imitating Beatles songs and then one Saturday afternoon, in the Harmony House (our local record store), I discovered this guy named Dylan. I wasn't even sure how to pronounce his name so for a while I called him "Dilen" with a long "I." The first Dylan record that I bought was entitled "Another Side." It was actually his third release. I had no idea that recordings were referred to as "sides" in the record business. I was just a kid in a record store so I took the title at face value.

This was folk music which was not at all what the Beatles were doing, which in retrospect might have been classified as just revved-up Buddy Holly, but at the time, I had no idea who Buddy Holly was. All I knew was that these two different genres of music had somehow stood in juxtaposition in my mind with no direct musical connection, at least not yet. I didn't know it at the time but in years to come all of this would have a dramatic impact on my work. I began to learn every song on that Dylan record, even imitating his nasal voice. Of course, he wasn't the kind of singer that could easily be compared to the Beatles but somehow his voice was compelling.

Back at Sacred Heart, I was now in sixth grade. There was no room in class for my love of music. Our class was possibly the largest class in the school, nearly forty kids in our room. Our teacher was Sister Anna Daniels. Because of her rather large aquiline nose she was nicknamed "Sister Anna Banana," but also because of her reputation as being a strict disciplinarian she was known to some as simply "Bulldog."

One day, in early fall, we were filing out of the classroom for recess. Because of the large number of kids, filing out was a big production requiring precise timing with almost military procession. Sister Anna for some reason thought that I was jumping line. Almost every Sunday I served as an altar boy, I always tried my best not to break the rules but still she singled me out. When we got out of the classroom into what was called the "Cloak Room" area she punched me right in the chest. I flew into the hard plaster wall and slid down dragging a coat or two with me. I totally lost my breath, kind of like when you fall out of a tree house. I was gasping for air and simply couldn't breathe. She was truly furious with me. I knew that I did nothing wrong and when I got home that day I told my mother that she had to get me out of this school or they were going to kill me. I remember thinking how this whole "love thy neighbor" stuff had suddenly stopped making any sense. My mother surprisingly succumbed and pulled me out of Catholic school and put me into public junior high. I suppose that maybe she caved in as a result of hearing so many stories about physical abuse at the hands of the nuns, or maybe she just thought about the money that she would be saving. Either way, soon enough I would be walking the halls of Memorial Junior High.

I no longer had to wear a uniform, I could mingle with kids who weren't necessarily Catholic and were hopefully different than the kids I was used to. "Different" for Vineland, New Jersey, in the sixties did not mean diverse. It just meant predominantly other white kids. We would gather in the school yard before the opening bell and try to blend. I met Alan Sugar, the son of a local doctor who, as it happened, played bass guitar. There was John Grassman, an artistic type who was an ardent fan of the same music that I was listening to and was also very interested in modern poetry. Finally, I was introduced to an underclassman named Arthur Ostroff who happened to play the drums. Somewhere in there, between Alan and Arthur was the beginning of my first band. It was almost as though the universe was conspiring in my favor. This handful of newfound friends would become a valuable support structure that I so desperately needed. John, however, would be the only one to become a lifelong friend.

John and I shared a love of language. We were both reading "free verse" poetry by writers such as E. E. Cummings, T. S. Eliot and others, and had already associated these poetic works with what Bob Dylan was doing at the time. Becoming exposed to all this new literary expression fueled my passion for reading. Even though I was a painfully slow reader, I had become a proud collector of books which would become a lifelong obsession.

This was the time of The British Invasion beyond the Beatles; suddenly we had the Rolling Stones, the Animals, the Zombies, The Kinks, and so many more. England just kept cranking them out. There was one new band however, that was tying it all together for me. A domestic west coast band called The Byrds had successfully fused the music of the Beatles and the work of Bob Dylan together into something that became known as "Folk Rock." They played Rickenbacker guitars just like the Beatles. The Byrds made the electric twelve-string a weapon to be reckoned with. That jangly ringing sound was their signature and it was extremely hypnotic. There was also a subliminal association between the tone of those Rickenbackers and the sudden interest in music from India. Ravi Shankar, India's most respected classical sitar virtuoso had become an overnight sensation. He gave sitar lessons to George Harrison of the Beatles.

In the wake of all this excitement, I formed my first band. Alan Sugar played bass, Arthur Ostroff was on drums, and I was resigned to sing and play my red guitar. John Grassman became the band historian. He had a small reel-to-reel tape deck and would record our rehearsals in Arthur's basement. My mother religiously subscribed to *Family Circle* magazine. There were copies of it lying about in our family room. The Byrds had used a "y" instead of an "i" in spelling their band name. Of course the Beatles were also clever in forming their "nom de plume." So I thought about "The Family Circle" being respelled as "The Famly Syrcle" and there it was, our new unstoppable identity. We were doing mostly Top Ten covers but we always tried to make them our own somehow, and not just a note-for-note knockoff. We were incredibly naive but intensely serious. We would be stars.

Things began to open up a bit socially at this point probably because of the band thing. I actually managed to get a
girlfriend. She had beautiful brown eyes the size of saucers
with long dark lashes. She sparkled even when her lips were
pouty. Her name was Jackie LaGuardia and she was hands
down the most beautiful girl in town. I had lucked out big-
time. I even got up the nerve to ask her to go steady and gave
her my confirmation ring. We would always make out in Arthur's basement when the band was taking a break from
rehearsal, which was almost always. So I guess it's really
true what they say about being in a band . . . you get the babes.

I didn't dress like everyone else. I took to wearing the
inside of my stadium coat as a vest and commandeering my
father's old forgotten neckties to decorate a paramilitary
shirt with shoulder epaulettes. When I wasn't busy getting
beaten up on my way home from school because I looked
different, I might be hanging out with John Grassman.
Sometimes we would hang out on weekends. Both John and
I were trying to get away with growing our hair a bit longer.
John was every bit as good a friend as Ed Dondero, just different. We would read the works of Ferlinghetti and Ginsburg
and have discussions about the imagery in works like "Howl"
and "Coney Island of the Mind." His mom and dad seemed to
like me and were always welcoming when I needed a break
from the anxiety at home. John was also learning how to play
guitar and we were both trying our best to write our own poetry. John often came up with shit that impressed the hell out
of me. He once wrote a piece that included the line, "if you're
not grateful, I'm sure the dead will be," a clever reference to
the band The Grateful Dead. I was so struck that I "borrowed"
his line for something that I was working on. Thankfully, he
found it in his heart to forgive me. I would often bring my

guitar to John's house and play for his father. His dad was a huge Johnny Cash fan and seemed to really enjoy hearing me sing and play my folkie Dylan stuff.

John and I would eventually wind up attending Vineland High School together. With all that was going on in the world I thought it would be really cool if we put out an underground newspaper. I had seen a few of those publications on a recent school trip to New York City when we visited the East Village. So John and I, along with one or two other contributors wrote articles as well as poetry for the publication, which was to be named *Satori,* a Zen Buddhist word meaning "sudden enlightenment." The last page of the five page mimeographed tableau included a short list of antidotes for quelling a bad acid trip. None of us had ever done LSD yet, but I thought that putting this information in the paper would make us look cool. I did some illustrations and after a few weeks we actually put this five-page tableau together. We actually convinced my drummer Arthur's mom to mimeograph the pages for us at her office and passed it out free of charge in the halls of the high school. We all used biblical names to disguise our identities. I was Moses and John was Noah. One article in particular got the faculty's attention. It was entitled the "VHS Mustache" (Vineland High School). It basically addressed the silently accepted practice of what we perceived to be an inequity in our school. Race relations in general were a red-hot topic in the mid-sixties, so everyone was extremely sensitive when anyone stirred up some dust, back in '67. The black boys at our school were permitted to grow facial hair. It seemed to us that the faculty was reluctant to ask them to shave, not wanting to provoke discord. We had no problem with other students' mustaches or beards but we wanted to be able to have them as well. Our article infuriated some black faculty members. It wasn't our intent to drive a divisive wedge into the issue but simply to see it worked out in a fair and equitable manner. We were wide-eyed, idealistic, pubescent, and we wanted facial hair! We were also quite innocent.

By third period the voice of Mr. Mancuso, the principal, came booming over the school public address system demanding by name that we appear in his office immediately. We were threatened with expulsion but Mancuso calmed down as he actually began to look at the tableau. A slight smile came to his face as if to say that he empathized with our sense of rebellion. Standing up, Mr. Mancuso said, "You must never pass out a publication like this on school property ever again!" Finally, he dismissed us from his office. He allowed everyone to leave except for me. When we were alone, he put his hand on my shoulder and looking me straight in the eye and said, "I really think that you should find somewhere else to go to school next year." He sensed that I was the ringleader and therefore I was a pariah. Luckily no word of this ever reached my mother. The principal never called my house, although this sort of thing would become a recurring theme throughout my education. I was trouble.

As the school year was ending, John and I decided that we would ask our parents if we could join the local theatre company. The Little Theatre of Vineland had a summer program that catered to kids like us. We were the local freaks, the outcasts, the kids who actually had talent, and the Little Theatre out on Sherman Avenue opened its doors to the lot of us. They would produce a revival of a Broadway musical during the break and both John and I thought it would be fun to try our hand.

The first production that we were in was a revival of *Carnival!* I played a roustabout, a part with no lines, more like a background character. The second show was *The Ugly Duckling* by A. A. Milne. I read for the part of the Prince which was the lead role and somehow got it. We went into rehearsals, which was drudgery for me. I wanted instant gratification and rehearsals just didn't offer that; so I would simply phone it in. I just hated it. Our director, a kindly older woman named Aggie Nott, noticed this and it concerned her. Word got back to me of her dissatisfaction so I tried to beef things up a bit, but I still hated rehearsal.

Finally came our one and only dress rehearsal. My costume included green tights. Afterwards, I noticed the director quietly chatting with John and occasionally glancing in my direction.

A bit later John pulled me aside saying, "Hey listen man, Aggie says that you have to wear a jockstrap."

"What?!" I blurted.

"Yeah Gary, she's seeing a little more than she wants to."

We were opening the following night. I explained the issue to my mother who snickered at my situation and relented to run into town the next day and buy me an athletic supporter.

The next night was our premier and the house, small as it was, was packed. Naturally I was nervous especially about remembering my lines. I was beginning to regret my lackluster rehearsals and how I should have tried so much harder. Now it was "crunch" time and anything could go horribly wrong. Somehow, and for whatever reason, when I hit the stage I came to life. The performance was vastly different than the rehearsals. Somehow I not only took over the stage but totally ruled it as well. I suppose in retrospect, I was finally receiving the gratification that I had been missing. I could feel the energy in the room coming from both the audience as well as the other members of the cast. It was intoxicating. Afterward,

Aggie came over to me, hugged me, and congratulated me on a great show. She also jokingly added how worried she was that I would just phone it in like I did the rehearsals. Aggie, me, and my now securely harnessed "bait and tackle" were all greatly relieved. More importantly though I had found a source of love. Empty and fleeting as it was, it still filled me and fueled me. The feeling I was able to absorb from the audience felt like love to my teenage soul, filling the voids and giving me a warmth that was missing in my toxic vacant home. It was that feeling that would compel and inspire me to pursue a life on stage. In endless search for validation and love that I needed to become whole.

CHAPTER 3

THE VELVET PRISON

The holiday season was fast approaching and I was already campaigning for an amplifier so my guitar could actually be heard. Alan Sugar had an extra channel in his bass amp that I would plug my guitar into but I really needed my own rig. My mother was planning to have Thanksgiving at our house. This meant that Aunt Marie and my Uncle Tony would be coming over. It was always a different house when Aunt Marie was around and I really loved Uncle Tony too. He and his two brothers owned a hatchery in Minotola the next town over. Aunt Marie was their bookkeeper. They were in the baby chick business and were pretty successful at it. I remember hearing stories of how he and his brothers hosted Japanese workers at various times of the year, as they were experts at "sexing" the chicks.

Thanksgiving day was finally upon us. For Easter my mother would usually make a giant canned Polish ham; for her that was easy. Thanksgiving was another thing. I think that this might have been her first turkey and I could tell that she was nervous and very unsure of herself. Although she wasn't particularly fashion conscious, she bought herself a new brown patterned dress for the occasion. Leaning on the kitchen counter she studied her Betty Crocker cookbook, bouncing the big toe of her right foot on the floor with her glasses firmly planted on the tip of her nose. Finishing a cigarette, she mumbled to herself as her index finger moved across the page. I heard car doors slam, then voices approaching. Aunt Marie and Uncle Tony yelled, "Hello!" as they let themselves in.

My parents always kept liquor in the house though they rarely drank, but when Aunt Marie and Uncle Tony came over everybody had a few, even my mom, although I think she only drank tiny glasses of sweet vermouth.

Uncle Tony drank beer. So when my mother asked me to get him a Ballentine's I was all too happy to oblige my favorite uncle. I went to the cabinet and got a tall glass, filled it with ice, and poured it full of beer. I was so happy to have family around that I didn't mind pitching in even if it was something that I had never done before. I was walking it over to Uncle Tony when my mother, losing any sense of composure, began screaming at me. "That's NOT how you drink BEER!!!" she yelled, sounding fiercely annoyed. My uncle reassured her that it was all right, trying to calm her anger, but she wouldn't have it. She was furious. I imagined that her over-reaction was due to the stress of making that gigantic meal. She really had gone all out. Dinner had included everything one might expect at Thanksgiving: green beans, mashed potatoes, cranberry sauce, biscuits, and of course, a very big turkey. She was a better baker than a cook so she had also made several pies and even her special coffee cake with ground coffee mixed into the vanilla icing. Even with all this momentary delight, a high level of toxicity had gradually engulfed our household, as her nervous vibes couldn't help but prevail over the festivities.

It was well into the holiday season and the entire atmosphere was getting exponentially worse by leaps and bounds. Everything was restricted. I couldn't even put trash in the bin in my own bedroom. Screaming at me, she insisted that I walk any trash to the kitchen so my bedroom bin was always clean. Little did I suspect that things were about to take a very dramatic downturn. One afternoon just before Christmas vacation, I had just gotten home from school, and no one was there. I opened up one of the kitchen cabinets to get a snack but had opened the wrong one. Instead of Cheese Doodles, I found vials upon vials of pills. I had just stumbled upon my mother's secret stash, stuffed full of Biphetimine T 20's (black beauties), Dexedrine, Benzadrine, Yellow Jackets, Eskatrols, Nembutals, Seconals, Tuinols, and Quaaludes. The cabinet was stuffed full. I stood there in awe.

This discovery filled me with dreadful fear. I was a teenager. I didn't know as much about drugs as I thought I did but I knew enough to realize that these things were dangerous, even potentially deadly. I had heard about people using downs to commit suicide or stories about someone having a heart attack from an amphetamine overdose. Here she was, my mother, given to worry about me trying marijuana yet she was taking a bunch of this stuff every single day. It became crystal clear to me why my mother's behavior was so out of control. She could be speeding all day and then needed barbiturates to come down at night. I was spinning and I had no idea where to go with this shocking news.

As part of her mania, she had also developed a habit of "saving up" her anger. I didn't recognize the pattern until one afternoon when I was just a week shy of fifteen, naked and headed for the one shower that I was allowed to soil. At the end of the hall leading from my bedroom, I peered around the corner to see if my mother was nearby. I used my arms and hands to cover myself up. I just wanted to make a quick dart to the bathroom, but I needed to pass by the entry to the kitchen in order to do that. Everything seemed quiet. "Maybe she's in the family room or down in the basement working," I thought. So I went for it. Suddenly my mother appeared running toward me with one arm raised high clutching a wooden yardstick. She had ambushed me and began screaming wildly as she beat me with that measuring wood. I screamed out, "What's wrong with you?" but her answer made little sense. She began to rattle off a long list of infractions and punctuated each one with a swat of her stick. The intelligible bits of what she said I could barely recall because they were from so long ago. I then realized that she had done this sort of thing before. She was clearly out of touch with reality. When it was over I stumbled into the shower and cried. I was hurting deeply inside. The person that I depended on for safety had become my accuser. I was truly alone.

My father was staying out on the road later and later and leaving me with the responsibility of looking after my mom. I guess he just couldn't deal with the way things were going. He was a coward of sorts and avoidance was his only means of self-preservation. As for me, it never occurred to him that I mattered.

I needed to divert my own attention away from what was happening at home so it was around this time that I began to try to write my own songs. I had become fairly proficient at guitar, and my voice wasn't too bad. I was more than able to hit the notes, had a pretty good range, and I was getting creative ideas. Aunt Marie had gotten me a little tape machine so I began using that to get my ideas down. I never did manage to learn how to read or write music so having a tape recorder was a lifesaver.

In a matter of a few months I had managed to write three or four songs. There was a little coffeehouse called Grandma's in Glassboro, New Jersey, right near the local college. It was about a thirty-minute drive.

I honestly don't remember who drove or how we got there but a bunch of us piled into a car with the intention that I would perform my new songs. None of us had made arrangements with the establishment ahead of time so it was up to my friends to convince the owner that he should allow me to play. There weren't many patrons there that night so he agreed.

They had a small riser for a stage, nothing fancy, and I just sat on a bar stool with my guitar and microphone. I started into my four song set with all the wild abandon that I could muster. It was almost like opening night back at the Little Theatre. I found my power in the audience. That old familiar feeling began to fill my soul again. Naturally my friends were all applauding and cheering me on but when I finished the owner walked right up to me. He looked me straight in the eyes and actually put his waving finger in my face saying, "Don't you EVER stop doing this! I mean it! NEVER stop!" I agreed, but man was I shocked. This full-grown adult who had probably seen it all, actually took the time to impress this on me. My first performance in a solo setting had put a fire in my belly. I felt special, and accepted in a way that I had never felt at home. I wanted more.

It was now early spring of my sophomore year and I had a job at a local burger joint and would work after school and on weekends. I saved as much money as I could, and bought a decent used car. It was a 1964 Rambler Classic with burgundy paint and black interior. The coolest thing about this car was that the entire front seat folded back, turning the car into a virtual bed. For a kid my age this was a vehicle sent from heaven.

I mulled over the situation at home and knew that I had to get out. I began to think about putting some more of my "burger" money toward going to a boarding school, just to get out of my house. I talked to my parents about it and to my surprise they were very receptive. They even suggested that they would match whatever money I came up with to help pay for tuition, which puzzled me. This was an about-face from their typical frugality. Just the week before one of the guys I worked with at the burger place, a friend from Sacred Heart Elementary named Jimmy Seeds, and I were both getting off our shift. I accidentally put a dent in his car as I was pulling out. We had hung out together when we were younger so we just laughed about it and I said that I would take care of the repair out of my pocket so he wouldn't have to make an insurance claim. My mother always hated me tying up the house phone. "What if there's an emergency?!" she would yell. Jimmy called to ask about his reimbursement. While I was on the phone she walked up behind me and snapped, "Who's that on the phone?!"

"Mom, it's Jimmy Seeds, he's calling about the forty five dollars I owe him for denting his car," I said, covering the receiver. She literally grabbed the phone from my hand and screamed, "Jimmy, he won't be paying you anything!" and hung up on him with a slam. This guy was my friend; I felt just terrible. What the fuck was wrong with her?

Most of the time they were way beyond frugal, more than cheap, and now they were offering to spend money to send me away? Was there some hidden message here? Was there something going on in the shadows that I wasn't permitted to see? Of course this meant that I would be leaving my friends behind, but I would also be leaving this toxic home behind as well. That was something that I felt increasingly desperate about. My mother's prescription drug use certainly explained a great deal, but unfortunately dealing with her dramatic mood swings was untenable. I was pretty much on my own.

What kept nagging at me was that my parents seemed to be so receptive to the idea of me going away to school. Maybe they honestly thought that a good prep school might be an opportunity for me to succeed. Or maybe they just wanted me gone. Either way, we began looking at a few highly respected schools; first on the list was the Hill School in Pottstown, Pennsylvania, then Lawrenceville and last The Peddie School, which were both in the Princeton area of New Jersey. All the while we were looking at schools, I was sensing something strange coming from them. They were being too nice.

CHAPTER 4

PEDDIE LARCENY

I took the entrance exam for Peddie alone in a small room that was sparsely furnished. It looked something like a faculty lounge. There was a coffeemaker, some closets, a plain hardwood table, and a few chairs. I could smell the musty odor coming from the half-drawn drapes hung on the windows. The Peddie school was established in the mid 1800's. Its once modest grounds were originally a seminary for women but by the time I got there its sprawling campus, with its austere historic halls and softly rolling greens by Peddie Lake, hosted only boys. Very rich, entitled boys.

Somehow, I miraculously passed. I thought I was a goner for sure but either I actually nailed it or they just wanted that last-minute tuition money. As I recall, that was about $3,500 a year. I had only managed to save up $1,500 so my parents came up with the balance. I still couldn't figure out why. This was an Ivy League prep school to which I was now accepted. It seems strange when I think back on it. I knew at the outset that I didn't belong there, or more specifically, I would not easily be accepted as the "free spirit" that I was.

Peddie like most other prep schools of its kind, was not fo-
cused on the "individual" but rather the "status quo." One was
expected to fit in, to conform to the academic landscape, and
that was not me. Now I was faced with an even more stringent
environment than I had ever experienced in parochial school.
The blazer was back, so was the shirt and tie, corduroy pants
and penny loafers. I had signed myself into a new, very ex-
clusive hell. This was a school whose "Honor Society" was its
own version of Yale's "Skull and Bones." I would eventually
find that out the hard way. Peddie's Honor Society clandes-
tinely ruled the student body, meeting and operating in secret.
Young men from families infinitely more wealthy than mine
flanked me. Families, who wanted nothing more than to put
their own kids out of the picture, simply sent them away for
someone else to raise and mold into the next generation of
wealth and power.

One such example was Steve Knoph, heir to Knoph publishing, another was Russell Sarnoff, the grandson of David
Sarnoff who founded the RCA Corporation, the list went endlessly on. The year was 1967 and I was now sixteen years old.
The world was in turmoil, the Vietnam conflict was raging,
Jimi Hendrix was ruling the psychedelic movement, and I
was in a place where you were called aside because your side-
burns were too long.

I wasn't assigned to live in one of the dormitories, instead I
was placed in a house that was owned by the school and situated at a corner of the campus. I shared a drab modest room
with John Roberts, from Virginia. We enjoyed the luxury of
two single beds, two chests of drawers, and two small desks.
The house was shared with about six other students. We had
a rather stern housemaster, Mr. Lawton, who was like many
of the faculty, unmarried, and likely a closet homosexual.

The first order of business was to find some friends, kindred spirits. One of the first friends that I made aside from my roommate John, was a guy who also lived in the house. His name was Ed Maclin but everyone called him "Oz." I later found out that he had earned this nickname because he was a science and math whiz. Oz was thin, blonde haired, and looked like he had just escaped Haight-Ashbury. His family had a farm in Ringoes, New Jersey, where they kept horses. He would go home for a weekend with two tins of ordinary nutmeg and return to school with about five grams of amphetamine sulphate, which he extracted from the spice. This guy had figured out how to make speed and was working on synthesizing mescaline. Oz and I became pretty good friends. One weekend he invited me home to the family farm. On Saturday morning he suggested that we saddle up the horses and go riding into the hills with his father. His dad worked as a stockbroker on Wall Street in Manhattan. He could roll a cigarette on horseback with one hand. They gave me "Peanut," the biggest horse that I had ever seen. Oz and his father rode off thinking that I was behind them but Peanut, who was the size of a small pachyderm, wouldn't leave the corral. He just kept circling and circling then suddenly put his head way up in the air and headed full steam for the barn. This horse could barely get in or out of the barn without lowering his head so with me in the saddle I knew that catastrophe was afoot. I had to quickly decide whether to crouch down and hug the horse hoping that I would make it in or grab on to the top of the barn door and let the horse go out from underneath me. I chose the latter, managing to get my feet out of the stirrups just as Peanut was reaching the door. I grabbed on to the top of the barn door and fell on my back onto a cement slab. I was okay, just startled mostly, but I had certainly made the right choice.

After getting up and brushing off I walked into the barn and looked up at the hayloft where I saw tenpenny nails coming through the ceiling. Had I held on to the horse I would have surely been shredded. Although it was obvious that the Maclin family was well off, they were still very down to earth. I was struck by the warm relationship that Oz had with his parents, especially with his dad. I was secretly jealous.

At the end of that school year it was Oz who convinced me to go to an awards assembly that I was about to blow off. As it turned out, my name was called as the recipient of the Carl E. Geiger Poetry Award for contributions that I had made to the school's literary magazine, *The Amphion*. I had submitted a couple of short free verse poems as well as a ten page long poem entitled "Sonfish," which attempted to make a statement regarding the effects of advertising on society. Being recognized for these works meant a lot and was quite validating for a young nonconformist.

Back in the first semester of the year, long before my poetry win, I discovered that there was actually someone enrolled there who I already knew from my hometown. James Love was my contemporary and hometown neighbor. His father owned a jewelry store in nearby Hammonton, and I had actually ridden my bike to his house a few times as a boy back home in Vineland. At Peddie, he became something of an anchor for me. He and Oz were the guys who recognized and supported my creative side, my edginess, bought into my maniacal schemes, and ultimately accepted me for exactly who I was.

Every drug imaginable was available on this campus of rich boys. I bought my first hit of acid just before Halloween from Russ Sarnoff whose famous grandfather founded RCA. He was kind enough to come and find me to make sure that I was okay as I lay on my back taking in the autumn air, hanging out under a local bridge just off campus. I had taken a fairly decent dose about an hour earlier which hadn't kicked in, that was common for a first timer, so Russ came by with some weed thinking that it might be needed to kick-start the trip, and he was right. One hit of Honest to God "Panama Red" and my 1200 micrograms of Lysergic Acid Diethylamide-25 immediately let loose and it was spectacular. Everything around me was pulsating and fully bathed in light. Even the bridge that I was lying under became worthy of the most meticulous architectural appreciation. I was fascinated by the curvature of its span and the antiquated industrial look of the steel support. Everything that my parents feared was indeed happening.

Jimmy Love became a close confidant, which I desperately needed in this new "fertile wasteland." One weekend the school held a quasi-philosophical symposium which a few ardent existentially minded students attended. James and I went, as did a few other students who represented the invisible underground of the school, whose numbers were growing. The actual event was not much to speak of but we emerged as a group that became known as the "God Squad." A phrase turned on the old "Mod Squad" TV show, we became the "Merry Pranksters" of Peddie, modeling ourselves after Ken Kesey's crazy cohorts. Drug-fueled practical jokes of immense proportion became our specialty and trademark.

Somehow, James knew a way to get us into the campus chapel. The building was being refurbished at the time and there were construction supplies outside. We were interested in the bricks. We snuck into the chapel at about three in the morning and covered the entire pipe organ with those bricks.

Both keyboards upper and lower as well as all the bass foot pedals were meticulously covered with bricks depressing every single key. We switched on the organ and ran for our lives. Farmers from fifty miles away were complaining to their local newspapers that their cows were woken up in the middle of the night by a rumbling sound that no one could identify or explain.

Those mysterious noises and alarmed cows weren't enough for us . . . we had even more insidious plans.

Most of the teachers at Peddie lived in houses supplied by the school that were just off the main campus. The faculty's cars were easy prey as the teachers mostly neglected to lock them at night. We gathered about seven "squadies" together and targeted every vehicle. We put them in neutral and in the middle of the night, pushed them to the green at the center of the campus where a flagpole stood. We managed to chain the cars' bumpers together and then chain them all to the flagpole. When the faculty woke up, their cars were gone from their driveways and were being held hostage on the "campus green."

Then came the piéce de résistance, which involved newly installed turf on the lacrosse field. We went out once again under the cover of night to where the virgin turf lay in waiting and rolled it up tight. We then transported it to the marble floor of the rotunda of the main building. In the morning, students were arriving for their classes to find that there was now a lawn installed on top of the marble floors in one of the oldest buildings on campus, where most classes were held. We were on a roll. We were the underground and we were kicking some serious ass. The "God Squad" had struck! This was all quite exhilarating until we got caught.

One late November afternoon as I languished on my bed, someone whom I had never seen before appeared at my door. He had come to tell me that I was to appear that very evening before the "Honor Society."

"Oh . . . this can't be good," I thought.

They were mostly seniors, maybe seventeen years of age, but make no mistake, they were seriously in charge and I had some "serious behavioral problems." Was this going to be all about the Peddie chapel and the organ thing? I didn't think that anyone found out about that. Or was it about bringing all the turf into the rotunda? That one might have leaked out.

One afternoon, a month or so earlier, I had dropped some acid. This time, about 3000 mics. A double hit. There was at least four inches of newly fallen snow outside. I had gotten out of the shower all wet and steamy and noticed that the bathroom windows were very tall and low to the floor. You could open the window and actually step outside onto the narrow ledge that the roof provided. I wondered what it might feel like to trample on the ledge naked in the snow, so I stepped outside. When I saw our housemaster Mr. Lawton coming up the walk and spotting me there, I realized that maybe this wasn't such a good idea. I ran. He went hunting through the house, talking to the others, moving furniture around determined to find me. I burst into Oz's room on the top floor. He was actually asleep on his bed in his underwear under an open window. Oz liked the cold.

I half woke him up saying that I needed to hide in his closet. He opened one eye, motioned with his hand and rolled over. So there I remained completely naked for at least forty-five minutes until Mr. Lawton decided to leave the house and report me to Dean Shumman.

So maybe they had heard about that. God knows everybody else had.

In any event, a few hours later, I found myself standing before the most right-winged, boneheaded bunch of white power, neo-Nazi, butch-cut boys in blazers that I had ever seen. For nearly an hour I was grilled with insinuating questions and sarcastic comments. Their intent was clearly to intimidate, to break me down and make me feel small. After the last round of verbal abuse, I was informed that it would be in my best interest if I did not return to The Peddie School after Christmas vacation. Their spokesman ended the meeting with a simple, "You may go."

How could I tell my parents about this? I had only been there three months and I was already getting the boot!

I needed to find a way to appeal to my mom. Although all of this was clearly my own doing, I needed to create a story that she could get behind. She was actually pretty good at getting me out of things when I got into a pinch. Like the time a year or so earlier when I downed two of her quaaludes, drank a half bottle of wine, and decided to drive over to see my speed freak girlfriend in nearby Millville. I was seeing quadruple as I turned the corner onto Main Street. It was like choosing door number one, number two, or three. Naturally I picked door number four and hit a parked car and then left the scene of the accident. A double crime. I arrived at my speed freak girlfriend's house, burst into the living room, and gleefully began to strip off my clothes. She had the good sense to call my parents. She was mainlining crystal meth and she still had the wherewithal to call for help.

My mother spent the next afternoon at the Millville Police station getting me out of a serious vehicular violation.

She was good at that. Now what? My mother was not as upset about this as I had expected, instead she had a look of determination on her face. She wasn't about to be pushed around by a bunch of preppies, the petulant sons of rich people; she needed better than that and so demanded to meet with the Headmaster. She really surprised me this time. Man was she pissed but for once, not at me. My father and I sat in the car while this meeting took place. He was silent as usual, and picking up a newspaper from the backseat he began to read. She was in there for quite a while. Of course, I was thinking the longer the better, she must really be making her case. Her favorite TV show after all was "Perry Mason." So I was hoping that she might be able to infuse her meeting with Mr. Mason's ingenious legal skills. I believe that in these never-ending moments of silent waiting I came to the realization that maybe she had finally given up trying to control me. Her air of intent as she stormed off to meet the Headmaster was palpable.

When she emerged from the main hall and got into the car, clutching her purse she said, "They have agreed to let you stay as long as you begin seeing a psychiatrist immediately."

I suppose I had finally achieved the most coveted status of "menace to society." I was both terribly ill behaved and bat shit crazy as well.

CHAPTER 5

MIRRORS

The only true and reliable medical or psychiatric care was located in nearby Philadelphia. My family was already familiar with the Medical Tower, a building that rented to doctors of all kinds from general to specialists. It was the place where my mother brought me as a child to try and understand my voluminous and relentless allergies. At that time the "allergy test" procedure of the day was to soak a number of stiff, very sharp needles into representatives of nearly every possible allergen on the planet. The doctor would then make a scratch on my back with a needle soaked with one compound, then another and another, each needle representing a different candidate. There were times that I would leave there with as many as twenty-four deep visible scratches on my back.

A week later I would return to have the appearance of those scratches evaluated as positive or negative. This was a process that, as I recall, took about three months, at the end of which the physician presented his findings. His conclusions were actually bound like a hardcover book. In my particular case, a very thick book. Apparently, I was allergic to just about everything and my related asthma was very real. Although, my mind raced back to my mother's insinuation upon leaving that creepy house on Roberts Boulevard when I was little, because nowhere in that list of allergens did it make any mention of bricks. I was definitely not allergic to bricks. Otherwise, you name it. Coffee, tobacco, sugar, lactose, chocolate, tomatoes, and the list went on.

Before she knew it my mom was hunting down every can of goat's milk that she could find. She found maybe three.

So here we were again, only under vastly different circumstances this time. My mom had found a shrink for me, and his name was Dr. Avner Barcai. He was a very nice man whom I liked almost right off. As a doctor of psychiatry, he specialized in dealing with children and young adults like me and their problems. He was Israeli, spoke with a bit of an accent, and was more interesting to talk to than anticipated. Over the coming months we would meet every Saturday. At first I was hesitant to open up to him. In fact, there were those awkward moments when I would be sitting there trying to pour my heart out only to look up and suspect that he was merrily doodling on his legal pad. He eventually gained my complete trust by accepting a well-rolled joint as a gift to start off each session. I realized later that he most likely discarded them. Eventually my mother found out and her immediate reaction was to assume that I was now my shrink's drug dealer, and then totally freak out accordingly. There was a culmination to this process. It was nearing the end of the school year. I had fulfilled my end of the bargain. I would likely be moving on as a graduated junior from The Peddie School with the footnote that I never return. This would also end my time with Dr. Barcai, which was bittersweet because he had decided to return to Tel Aviv. The time that we had spent together turned out to be much more meaningful than I would have ever initially imagined.

Dr. Barcai suggested for the last session that all of us gather together with him. He spoke to us all briefly, describing the experiment that he wanted to try. He put my parents into a room with a couch and coffee table which had a one-way mirror installed on one wall. The doctor and I went together into an adjacent room where we could watch my parents without being seen by them. There were microphones and speakers in each room and he could talk with them as well as hear their responses. He began his questioning slowly in a gentle tone as to not ruffle any feathers. Eventually he dug much deeper by asking questions like "Did you or do you ever hug him?" "Do you ever tell him that you love him?" "Do you try to make him feel that he is special, or that he is loved?" At first it seemed that they didn't know how to respond, almost like they didn't know what he was talking about. What happened next I could hardly believe.

My parents were suddenly reduced to emotional rubble. They were both crying with their hands covering their faces. One minute they appeared just fine and the next completely decimated. I had never ever seen my parents this way. They were both in tears and I mean gut-wrenching tears answering, "No! . . . No!!" to his questions. I was stunned.

This interlude had gone on for more than fifteen minutes when he turned to me and said, "Gary, this is what you will have to let go of in order to live your life." This was the baggage that I would eventually have to leave behind. This gigantic emotional boatload of bilge that I needed to purge, including all the years of empty emotional support.

A few days after this event, I cornered my parents and actually asked them why they never gave me their approval for my musical ability. "We didn't want to give you a big head," was their response. "So instead you said nothing?" I screamed, searching for words. Hearing that made me incredibly angry. It was as though my parents were silently saying that they had no desire to be proud of me. I now understood that what Dr. Barcai had told me was indeed true. I had to somehow move on with my life and try as hard as I could to not let the gravity of this incident or how it would represent the past, affect or define me in any way. Easier said than done.

I managed to get a pass from The Peddie School but now my mother was getting more sick and unmanageable than she had ever been. I thought that it might be best to tuck my tail between my legs and move back home. My parents, not willing to admit to failure had enrolled me in Saint Augustine, a local prep school in Richland just outside of Vineland. Really that was my best and only choice. My parents seemed willing to pay for one final year of preparatory schooling and I would be right to simply go along with the plan. Back to Catholic school. Taught primarily by Augustinian priests and monks along with a few lay teachers, St. Auggie's was the cream of the crop as far as South Jersey was concerned. A very small school at the time, it had no athletic teams, no extracurriculars, yet it was well accredited and highly thought of within the local community. I think that when the faculty heard that they were about to get a "Peddie Boy" amongst their ranks, some of them got excited. A "Peddie Boy" was affluent, academic, and well behaved. Three things I definitely was not. I would ultimately let them down, although I actually started off fairly well. I found that the classes were much easier for me, the homework not so intense and laborious. Even though

I had been reunited with Ed Dondero and a few others from my Sacred Heart days, there came that pressing issue of "fitting in." If I was to have any kind of social life among these guys then I needed to blend in a bit, which actually meant "dummying down" some. I began as an overachiever, which was easy because I was ahead of their academic curve. Although once again I wound up just before the Christmas break in a similar situation as the one experienced just the year before. Only this time it was me who wanted to drop out. Instead of being nearly thrown out like the year earlier, I was then at a point where I felt I had enough of convention. I just wanted school to be over so I could pursue music as a career and wasn't able to justify spending all this time waiting it out. Nothing much had changed at home, even after that dramatic breakthrough in the shrink's office. Around Thanksgiving I announced to my parents and to the school's administration that I would be leaving.

I even found a place to live. Over the Woolworth store in Millville there was a giant empty loft space. The rent was affordable and I was thinking big. I could live there with my speed freak girlfriend and leave academia behind. Although the landlord didn't seem too keen on having undesirables there; "No Hippies," he snorted after showing me the place. Just the same, imagine, the whole top floor of a Woolworth store to live in. "And exactly where is this place?" my mother asked, in her smudged apron, dragging on a cigarette.

The next thing I knew, I was sitting in Father LaRosa's office waiting for my mother to arrive. Father LaRosa was the school's headmaster; his nickname was "Chick." What he might have done to have secured such a sobriquet was unknown to me. We waited for a while in silence. A silence that became thunderous.

I was just about to ask him about his nickname when he separated his fingertips and leaned toward me, resting his arms gently on the desk. "You started out strong here, young man," he said, "you could have been a fine student but then you began to 'flounder.'" Father LaRosa's lips kept moving but I didn't hear a word. My creative mind took over and suddenly a cartoonish image popped into my head. I morphed into a dripping wet, fat fish out of water, smoking a cigar, lounging on a chair in the headmaster's office with my fins gently flipping on the floor.

"Yeah Fatha," I would have said, "I'm a flounderin . . . " I digress.

It was raining as my mother's car pulled into the lot. She appeared at the entrance to the school just adjacent to Chick's office. She wore one of those plastic rain scarves that tied just under the chin, her cat's eye frames and face dripping wet from the downpour. As she came into Father LaRosa's office, I slipped my hands into my pockets gently gripping my imaginary weapon. They both did their best to try to convince me of how idiotic I was being. "You *are* being very foolish," my mother chimed in, "why would you drop out of school when you are so close to finishing?" In the end, no weapons were drawn. No shots fired, no bombs tossed. The "me-fish" image of myself now wanted nothing more than to simply swim away. They had used logic to break me down and they had won. Bastards! I gave up arguing, making a case for my desperately passionate bohemianism. Surrender was clearly the path of least resistance. Do the time and be done with it. So I resumed my education at Saint Augustine and would simply do the best I could until graduation.

When that day eventually came I was in complete elation. It was over. I was done. My commitment to society had been satisfied. My ticket punched and validated.

As we were all leaving the building on that afternoon I decided to duck into the faculty restroom because I really needed to take a piss.

When I came back into the hall, Mr. John Mahoney our self-aggrandized, balding-too-early-for-middle-age English teacher/latter-day, semi-modern poet was walking by the restroom door. He was self-published, not great stuff but published to be sure. He looked at me and sneered, "Mesiano, you're never going to amount to anything." *That sonofabitch!* I thought. Oh yes! For using the faculty bathroom I indeed was the scourge of the earth, or so it seemed at the moment he saw me. I was the last dollop of useless bacterial swamp scum simply taking up surface space on the slippery side of the planet. If I had my mother's piercing, daggerlike eyes, I would have shot a million knives into his back. My rage overtook me and again my arcane imagination kicked in. As he lay there bleeding in the hallway, I would flash back to some Brando-like character from a fifties "Film Noir," leaning over him yelling, "Yeah you watch me, Mahoney. I'm gonna prove to you and every other bastard out there who thinks I'm a worthless piece of shit that I AM worthy. I'm going to BE somebody. You just WATCH me."

In recent years I have actually seen John Mahoney on local south Jersey television. He has become something of a "Cable TV Sommelier." His commercials pop up from time to time during late night and he gives some seemingly "solid advice" on the consumption of what he considers to be wine of a finer vintage. I wonder if he knew what I had become? Had he ever seen me on MTV, or heard my music? Did he know that I penned a Grammy Award-winning song? Did it really matter?

At the beginning of summer after graduation I was happy that my part-time job at Garwood Mills, a local department store, would now become full-time. I managed the candy department and also the record department. For me, this was very cool. I could play with vinyl all day long. I was never someone who actually went in for sweets all that much except for maybe Peanut M&M's, but handling the record department was really fine. Jimi Hendrix had died at the beginning of the school year and I was terribly crushed. I was at the store that day after school when the news came over the radio. I actually called the local station to make sure that I wasn't hearing things. Luckily all was not lost, and there was still tons of great music out there. I remembered just the year before when my old friend John and I stumbled upon Johnny Winter's first record. The Harmony House would let you preview new releases and even had dual headphones hooked up to the turntable. I dropped the needle on that disk, we looked at each other and gulped to ourselves, "Holy shit!"

Summertime was always concert time and there were a lot of great concerts going on that summer. My friend Arthur and I drove to Philly one night to see Johnny Winter perform at the Electric Factory. That's when he was doing the "Johnny Winter And" thing, which included Rick Derringer of "Hang on Sloopy" fame on guitar. What a killer show, but the biggest surprise was the opening act. Seals and Crofts was actually doing an acoustic set just before this super loud, guitar driven band.

The two of them came out with just a bass player supporting them and killed the room. They were nothing short of fantastic. Arthur and I even got to say hello to Dash Crofts when he popped out of the dressing room to check out Johnny. We were both really impressed and I was sure they would be stars. Their latest record, "Riding Thumb," had just been released on the Bell record label. When it arrived at the store, I gave it a very prominent place among the record bins. I used to make up little cartoonish signs that I would stick in the front of a bin holding a record that I particularly liked. I posted a really good cartoon sign for that record. I would continue at this job working hard through the fall. I had plans to leave sometime right after Christmas. I was just saving up money to make the move. My close friends were all beginning to sense that I really was going to keep my word and eventually leave. Naturally some of them said, "You'll be back" or, "Hey man, you're just gonna wind up living in my basement," or, "You'll be knocking on my door within three months!" It wasn't as though I had to prove them wrong but I instinctively knew that those words would never hold me back.

CHAPTER 6

MANHATTAN

The little blinking lights on the apologetic green artificial tree next to the piano in the family room made me think, for a fraction of a fraction of a second, that I might miss being home. This would be my last Christmas there. I sat down for a moment and placed my hands on the keyboard and then suddenly, that thought was gone. Surely, I would miss my mother's coffee cake, but that was about it. Even though as a child I was diagnosed with asthma I hadn't had an attack in ages. It was almost like my physical body had finally healed itself in preparation for its freedom. Just the same it was sad for me to reflect on all this. My mother's "condition" had gotten completely out of hand. Now it seemed that there was also something physically wrong that she kept to herself and I didn't ask. All I knew was that she had begun driving herself to the same Medical Tower in Philadelphia every Saturday and came home looking withered and pale. She had reached new heights of irritability, saying things that didn't make sense or referring to incidents that happened weeks before, things that didn't fit into any conversation.

Aunt Marie had a favorite phrase she used to describe herself on the brink of insanity, "fit to be tied," she would say. That was my mother. A massively fragile bundle of nerves that, if prodded, could explode at any moment. The memory of me dragging her nearly lifeless body across the floor that day a couple of years earlier, stole into my brain as I watched the lights on the tree blink over and over. Blink, blink, blink.

I would soon be free from this cushy velvet prison, free from overhearing my mother at the kitchen table telling my dad that she simply *must* have control over me. I would be free of her ransacking my room when I wasn't around, looking for things that I had written or anything that she could find to use against me. She would copy down her findings on an index card and place them in a small metal filing box. She might have been saving up her anger again and I must have done something to trigger her wrath. I remembered one night after dinner she demanded that both my father and I remain at the table after it was cleared. Reaching into the pantry cabinet she pulled out her little metal box. Opening it, she began going through the index cards and reciting the "inflammatory evidence" that she had uncovered. I would sit there completely stunned, then glance over at my father to see him staring down at the table as if wishing he was anywhere else. He was her audience for the inquisition. Rifling through my desk drawer she had found an unmailed letter that I had written to a girl in Canada. This poor girl from Alberta was a pen pal that I had found in the back of *Tiger Beat*, a teen magazine. We had written back and forth a few times but I had written her again, intending to post the letter but never did. In it, I boasted wildly about being disruptive in class. Of course I was more than exaggerating but naturally my mother assumed my words to be fact. I would sometimes imagine that I was actually in a scene from her favorite show "Perry Mason." Mason's detective, Paul Drake, would have me sitting under a hot lamp, interrogating me with a lit cigarette hanging from the corner of his mouth. "Well, I for one would really like to hear your explanation, Mr. Mesiano?" I was eighteen already. "Who lived like this?" I wondered.

My father was almost nowhere to be found. Even I was becoming suspicious. Some nights he wouldn't pull into the driveway until 9:00 PM or later. One night when he rolled in really late I heard my parents fighting. I snuck down the hall trying to get closer to the kitchen but I still couldn't make out what they were arguing about. Suddenly, my mom got into her car and drove away.

I started to wonder if my father might be cheating on her because she was so impossible to be around. If that were true, I really couldn't blame him. I was fairly sure that they hadn't had any "loving moments" in quite some time. A few hours later she returned and when she came into the house, trying to make things better I said, "I missed you." She seemed actually touched by the gesture and said in a small voice, "Thanks." She walked into her room and went to bed.

I really needed to make up my mind about exactly where I would be going. At first I thought of Philadelphia. There was a decent music scene there but it was just too close to home. Alan Sugar, my old bass player from the "Famly Syrkle" days, had a younger brother Bruce who moved to Nashville and was having some success as a recording engineer. This was still the "Old Nashville" and would be a music market to which I would have to conform. James Love, from my days at Peddie, had moved to LA, but I thought that California might just be a bit too far away from home. New York City was the only viable choice for me. It was a major music hub and still close enough to home to go back and visit if I wanted to. Just a little more than a two hour bus ride. That was it then, I had made my choice: New York City it was.

Sometime just after Christmas I informed my parents that I had no intention of going to college. I had not applied to any school and my parents had never mentioned it. One might think that after all that prep schooling the subject might have come up, but in fact they never even suggested. They never realized that it might have meant a coordinated effort between them and me to look into higher education. Neither of my parents had gone beyond high school. It was almost like they didn't mind so much that I wouldn't go to college. Yet when I told them, they feigned surprise.

"What? You mean you're not going to college?" my mother exclaimed. I had been hanging around the local AM radio station at night. I got to know the owner who eventually gave me a key so I could come by and practice reading the news from the Teletype into a tape recorder. Really what I was doing was coming in with a few of my friends and recording my songs on their equipment. My mother thought this was an opportunity to press me to get a broadcasting license. If I wasn't going to go to college then I needed something to fall back on, even though the license was nothing more than a "rubber stamp." After the new year, I studied the course and went to Philadelphia to take the test that would eventually grant me the license. I failed what was called "Element 9," the "tech" bit, which was all about what to do when the transmitter went down. As if I would actually climb the radio tower in a thunderstorm to fix the station's antenna. I studied some more, retook the exam, and passed. It seemed strange that you needed a license just to be an "on air" personality back

then that was the deal. I never used the rather official looking document, although I did slip it into a dime-store frame.

It was time to tell my parents of my plans to move to New
York City and get into the music business. My mother was neither happy nor supportive, which was not a huge surprise as
she was rarely happy or supportive. "No one just gets into the
music business!" she said snidely.

My mind was made up. I had to go. I needed to be far away
from this toxic situation. I asked them to drive me to New
York on Valentine's Day, only a week or two away. They reluctantly agreed, knowing that I had so much resolve that
I would simply get on a bus should they refuse to take me.
When that morning finally came my mother said she wasn't
going. I wasn't sure why she wanted to stay at home. Maybe
she didn't feel well or maybe she just couldn't bear to see me
go off into the sunset. She told me that my father would drive
me and would pick up Aunt Marie on the way and they would
take me to the city. I was packed and ready to go. My father
already had his coat on so I just walked over to my mother
and said something like, "This isn't goodbye . . . it's just . . .
goodbye." Her eyes began to well up and it was time to go.

The year was 1971, February 14th, Valentine's Day when
we drove off in my father's 1962 robin's egg blue Plymouth
station wagon. I rode shotgun and Aunt Marie held down the
backseat. We set off cruising through the long flat South Jersey landscape. I sat watching the pine barrens roll by in what
I thought might be my final farewell. Aunt Marie was never
too fond of my father. I think that she found Joe Mesiano to
be something of a braggadocio. Normally, he rarely said a
word but every so often, if he felt provoked or threatened, he
would suddenly be given to talking very big about himself,
trying to make himself more important than he actually was.

In reality, he probably had a terrible inferiority complex and maybe that's why he married my mother in the first place. He was stoically silent that day, displaying no emotion at all from his poker face. "Maybe the war had actually carved out his heart," I wondered. The air in that car was as thick as you might imagine. What would normally be a two and a half hour trip seemed endless.

Then all at once, New York's skyline became visible, rising out of the marshland looking like the Land of Oz. Skyscrapers piercing the sky like phalluses against the virginal heavens, they beckoned to me from a distance as my heart raced with anticipation. I was scared, excited, determined, and filled with wonder. My life, in earnest, was about to begin.

That Valentine's Day was crippling cold, the bone-chilling kind. Once we got through the Lincoln Tunnel and landed in midtown Manhattan, Aunt Marie called from the backseat for us to stop at the newsstand on the next corner. I jumped out and grabbed *The New York Times*. She began looking over the classifieds and after a few moments spurted out, "What about this place?" "The Hotel Lucerne at 79th and Amsterdam has small single rooms for $45 a week," Aunt Marie called from the backseat. "Can you manage $45 a week, Gary?" I had roughly $250 in my pocket so this would last me nearly a month. In 1971 Manhattan looked like a barren wasteland. Everything seemed jagged and grey. Steam rose up from the manhole covers forming ghostly clouds. You could almost feel the light of day trying to keep the shadows at bay. This would not be your classic "Leave the baby on the doorstep" moment, this was no Mary Tyler Moore intro, no beret hurled breathlessly into the air. I was the guy you might see in a movie standing in the street with his guitar and suitcase, staring up at the building where his new life would begin. Only there was no theme music, and all I had was what I brought with me plus two cartons of Marlboros that Aunt Marie had shoved at me saying in her gravelly voice, "Here . . . you're gonna need these." Standing there in my cable sweater and jean jacket, I was freezing my ass off. My father must have been feeling generous that day; he reached into his pocket and sprung for the first week's rent. He even walked me into the well-worn lobby and made the arrangements with the front desk. I thanked him, shaking his hand, and gave Aunt Marie a big hug, and standing in the hotel entrance watched them pull away. In retrospect, I was happy that they had driven me because as brave as I thought I was, it would have been so frightening to have gone it alone. My heart was in my throat. Had I made the right decision? I was now alone in the big city. Swallowing hard I tried to let any thoughts of self-doubt be gone.

I checked into the Hotel Lucerne with my guitar and suitcase filled with a week's worth of clothing, finally holding my room key to my new life in the palm of my hand. "I might as well go upstairs and get settled in," I thought. I was headed to a room on the second floor of this ten story building. I slipped the key in the door and voila. "Well this can't be much more than eight by ten," I said to myself aloud, surprised at the lack of grandeur within. Once inside I noticed that an entire chest of drawers had actually been shoved into a closet and there was a pitifully small sink on the wall at the foot of the bed. The good news was that I could use the windowsill as my fridge. I wound up keeping my milk, cheese, wine, and pepperoni out there. Down the hall I found a bathroom with several showers and toilets. I bought some thumbtacks and nylon string to set up an elaborate network of crisscrossing spiderwebs on the wall, so I could hang my clothes to dry

after hand washing them in the sink. It was a bit like camp-
ing but it worked. I could finally breathe into the moment.
I now had a certain handle on my albeit unknown destiny.

Arthur, my old drummer, had a cousin Alan who lived
somewhere in the city working for Epic records. Alan used to
work at Colony Records, which was the biggest retail record
store on Broadway, and he had mentioned to Arthur that I
could drop his name to get a job there.

That first week I went out every day looking for work. I
was hoping to find a job on my own without having to rely
on Alan's name. One would think that I would look for work
in a record store other than Colony. But no. I thought I could
work in a "head shop," a rather lofty aspiration but not so far-
fetched in that I already had vast experience in that sort of
thing.

Finally, after multiple turndowns, I caved and one morning found myself at the Colony store. I walked up to the
manager, explained who I was and that Alan could vouch
for me. Apparently he was well thought of, and suddenly I
had a job. I trained at the main Colony store but they also
had two satellite stores in the immediate area. One was
simply called "Nappy's," named after one of the partners
in the business who had extremely tight and thick curly
hair. I was assigned to work there for the curmudgeonly yet
softhearted Max Roth. The store, which was right next to
the Winter Garden theatre, opened at nine in the morning
and stayed open till late night to accommodate the tourists.
I was working a typical day shift, and just loved being around
records. It reminded me of the job that I had back home at
Garwood Mills, running the record department, but this was
so much bigger, and much more exciting. I was a clerk in the
biggest record store on the eastern seaboard.

After a few months the hotel began to get old and I was getting tired of washing my clothes in the sink. The bathroom at the end of the hall was pretty creepy. Just a short row of stall showers, toilets, and sinks. Thankfully I never saw anyone in there, just roaches. Everything was feeling small, like the walls of my little room were about to devour me. So I began to scour the newspapers for a possible roommate situation. I saw an ad for a single bedroom for $75 dollars a month in a five-bedroom apartment shared by four other people way up in Washington Heights. This area of Manhattan was practically "out of town," but the rent was less than I was paying at the hotel and I would have my own room in an apartment with two bathrooms and a kitchen. When I saw the place, it was pretty much a done deal. The apartments in that area of Manhattan were quite grand. In this particular flat the bedrooms were very big, plus there was a living room with a TV, a dining room with French doors, a bunch of loony roommates, and even a piano. It was a bit on the funky side but it felt just right, so I jumped on it. My new room was certainly more than big enough and had a nice sized closet. One of my roommates told me that the guy who lived there before me had wound up in a mental hospital apparently plagued by schizophrenia. There were industrial sized bottles of Thorazine, Stelazine, and other drugs in the room that he had left behind. That didn't bother me. I began painting the walls with murals of ships sailing the ocean. I even put some blue glass stain on my upper windows and used black electrician's tape to imitate solder. I wanted to put my own signature on the place. Just doing those frescoes was an act of sheer liberation. I could have never done that back home.

The only drawback of my new place was that it would now take me about an hour to get to work. I wasn't situated near an express stop so I had to take the local all the way. I would grab a coffee and pack a book and get on the train, prepared for the long ride to midtown. The local train would move mostly underground but there was a short run when the train went above-ground and ran above the street. Like a bridge it was supported by steel columns. In New York City terms, that was called an "El," short for "elevated." During those brief moments I could gaze out the train windows and instead of the blackness of a tunnel, I would see the sun illuminating the run-down neighborhoods of Hamilton Heights and Harlem. Occasionally, I could even see signs of life flashing by as the train shot downtown.

Colony as well as its two satellite stores were strictly high end retail, which basically meant that records were sold at "list" price, making it the most expensive record store in the city. It also boasted of being the place to find certain things that were very hard to come by, rare or even out of print. Those recordings demanded a rather hefty price tag. It was like the "Tiffany's" of record stores. Customers could walk in and I would actually wait on them, ask them what they might be looking for. If they were looking for something special it was my job to not only know what that record was but also where to find it in the vast library of vinyl that Colony controlled.

There was a large counter space that offered two turntables so that customers could preview records they were considering for purchase. This of course also meant that when things were slow, I could pretty much play any record that I wanted to hear. It soon became my job to receive and unpack all new releases. This was really exciting as I would be the first to hear anything brand-new and interesting. I could put on T. Rex or something by a new artist like David

Bowie who would become major influences. My head simply exploded when I played "Ziggy Stardust" for the first time, but I had to keep it down or Max would yell at me. I would then file each record according to its label and catalog number. We received two copies of everything new. One copy became the opened, filed and numbered copy, having its own custom sleeve, and the other would be a pristine factory-sealed copy of the same filed right next to it. The album cover for the "sleeved" copy was then placed out in the store bins. That was done not only to guard against theft but to ensure the personal service aspect of store policy. Any customer could just grab an album cover from a bin, bring it to the counter and I would give them the sealed copy. I would draw all kinds of designs on the opened sleeve copy just like I used to do back home working the record department at Garwood Mills. I learned how to keep the filing accurate and up to date. I was becoming something of a vinyl librarian, a walking encyclopedia of rock. I would unconsciously funnel much of what I was listening to into what I was writing at the time. That period of all the pre-disco recordings was like a gold rush of musical mining for me.

One morning around eleven or so, I was on my third coffee when in walked Rod Stewart with a nice looking, smoky-eyed blonde, possibly from the night before. He was very well dressed in a tailored shirt with a "high boy" collar buttoned at the top, no tie, wearing a "forest green" double-breasted corduroy suit. He walked right up to me and said that he was interested in looking for old 45 rpm's from the Stax and Volt record labels. He was shopping for some serious R&B.

He presented me with a list of titles and I began to scurry around the store looking for those 45s. I was able to find him just about everything that he was looking for. Then he started calling out titles off the top of his head. I combed through the shelves in the back room where all the "rare" records were stored. He must have chosen at least fifty singles. The order came with a hefty price tag as some of those 45s were out of print.

I was very pleased that Mr. Stewart was satisfied. As he and his friend stepped over to the cash register to pay Max, I glanced down at the counter to see his list of records still lying there. "Maybe I should have asked him to autograph it," I thought, still foggy from the whole experience. Without even realizing it, I had just had a "close encounter" with the future, so to speak. Of course, as soon as the door closed behind him I came to and screamed, "Holy shit! I just waited on Rod Stewart!!"

CHAPTER 7

FINDING DORY

On a rainy morning in early September the phone rang up in Washington Heights. One of my roommates took the call, then knocked on my door and somberly said, "It's for you."

"Hello," I said not knowing who to expect. "It's your father," said a distant voice, "I'm calling to tell you that your mother died last night." Naturally, I was stunned. I didn't expect it to happen so soon. I'm not sure that I expected it at all. Back in April I had taken the bus home for a weekend. Both of my parents had seemed happy to see me as I entertained them with stories from the big city. My mother seemed fine that weekend. In fact, much better than I had remembered. On the one hand, I still secretly despised her and on the other, she was the only mother I had ever known. Just a month earlier she had actually made the pilgrimage to New York to inspect my living situation; at that time she seemed really edgy. I think she was speeding heavily that day. It was easy for me to spot now. Her demeanor vaguely reminded me of the time she switched from cloth aprons to plastic ones. Her apron would make a "shu" sound as it cut the air when she would turn around quickly. After frenetically inspecting the entire apartment, including kitchen and bathrooms, she stood in the foyer asking sarcastically, "Who cleans?" Now she was gone.

I was nineteen years old when my father called me with the news. As he spoke, I flashed back to my childhood torment. There would be no more snide remarks, no more crushing questions, no more incriminating index cards. I was now free to walk on the plush carpet, even put trash in my bedroom bin if I wanted to. But I didn't want to do any of that now. I just wanted to understand the pain inside my chest. It was like a Molotov cocktail of both heartbreak and relief, working simultaneously to confuse and torture me. Of course I loved her. I just didn't know if it was the normal love a son has for his mother. I suddenly realized after all the years that I had spent dodging her anger that I actually had great compassion for her, but I never let myself be in touch with it. I was too busy protecting myself from what was happening to me. I now understood that she was her own victim and that self victimization was just one of the things she had taught me. Something that I would have to find a way to unlearn. The finality of her death meant that all that shit that I had tolerated was over. And while it was a great relief, I was still broken. Still untethered, I felt empty with no real connection to anyone on this planet.

I couldn't go home alone. I was just too emotional. I called a girl that I used to date when I was at Peddie. Joyce Passentino and I got very close during my year at the school. She was what we called a "townie," meaning she lived in town and had no connection to Peddie. We had stayed in touch even after I moved to New York. I told her what had happened and asked if she might be willing to come with me to the funeral in South Jersey. I barely slept that night. I was deep in mourning but still so torn at the same time. It reminded me of "Stockholm Syndrome" where the captive becomes enamored with their captor. Somehow I had managed to find some moments of solace while still living in her velvet prison. She had been at times so unkind to me, so unloving, and yet I still loved her deeply. This was crushing me.

I woke up the next morning to see Joyce already standing in my room. She was small of stature and very curvy, looking like a little cherub that had come to help. I put on some clothes and got myself together and we headed for Port of Authority to catch a bus to Vineland.

I can't even remember how I got to the viewing. I don't remember my father driving us. The viewing was held at Rone's Funeral Home. Most all of Vineland's Catholic families went to Rone's. The room was quite full. My father's family was huge, him being one of thirteen children. I could see all my aunts, uncles, and cousins and so many more that I didn't recognize. I remember all the flower arrangements around the coffin but I remember no music. I'm certain that there was music, I just couldn't hear it. My Ukrainian grandfather's second wife drove down from the Bronx with my mother's extended Ukrainian family, along with Aunt Marie, Uncle Tony, and his entire family. Thank God for Joyce. The casket had a deep sort of copper finish to it and I saw it as closed. Had my father not wanted to spend the money for embalmment or had something happened to her that no one was talking about? Here indeed was the strangest thing of all, because in actuality, her coffin was very much open. In fact there was a long anxious line of ghoulish people waiting to see her body. "How barbaric," I thought. I suppose my mind would just rather have seen it as closed.

It's strange to say but I don't actually remember my father even being there. I know of course that he was, and in fact I remember at one point standing right next to him and noticing how nicely he was dressed in a dark brown suit that I had rarely seen him in. We didn't say a word to each other. People and things began to irritate me. As I walked in from the foyer, my Uncle Sammy, my father's most boisterous brother, was standing by, when he saw me he howled, "Hey . . . haha . . . here's Gary . . . and it looks like he needs a haircut." That bothered me. Later, it was on to the funeral which was held at St. Isidore's, our new local Catholic church. This new church had been recently built to serve the parishioners who were living just beyond the reach of old Sacred Heart. It was of a contemporary design with "abstract" stained glass windows that finished off the modern touch. I remember the eulogy as being laborious and having no real connection with the person my mother was. Ed Dondero's mother, who was sitting right behind me, poked me in the back urging me to sit up straight, and that bothered me. Later at the Oak Hill Cemetery I watched as her coffin was slowly lowered into the ground; she was buried right next to my Ukrainian grandfather. As everyone walked to their cars, my grandfather's second wife pushed my shoulder with a grunt, "Go be with Marie!" That really irritated me. "Who are these fucking people?" I thought. But I dutifully obeyed and made an effort. Still, I was in pretty bad shape. She had lost her sister, and I had lost my keeper. That night, Joyce and I stayed in my old bedroom. It would be the first time I shared my childhood bed with anyone. The next day I vaguely remember saying goodbye to my father. Joyce and I got a bus to New York and she stayed with me for a day or two, which was just what I needed. She was a sweet soul who always got me to smile. Somehow she instinctively knew the path to my heart. I let myself bathe in her kindness, trying to heal myself of this sudden new reality.

In the aftermath of my mother's passing, once again the thought of finding my birth mother emerged in my head again. Was I now really free to really start looking for her? I had always sensed from my adoptive mother that my adoption was something that she wanted swept under the rug like it never happened. Maybe that's why she told me that my real mother had died giving birth. To her thinking, that image would close the book, so to speak. I could have no more questions. She would be completely wrong about that.

I heard in passing from someone at the funeral that Uncle Tony was sick. I remember him not looking very well when I saw him there. Apparently he had already had part of his stomach removed. I knew that he smoked a lot and had contracted emphysema, an ailment that I didn't know very much about. I had no idea how bad it was. A few months went by when I got another phone call from my father. He was calling to tell me that he was selling the house, as well as all of my belongings which also meant all of my beloved books.

"Why? . . . why my books?" I cried in despair. Despite my dyslexia, I had always been an avid reader and had plenty of books to prove it. I had built up quite a collection. So this news meant that my set of Funk & Wagnell's encyclopedias would be gone along with my rare leather-bound edition of Bunyan's *Pilgrim's Progress*, as well as so many other wonderful volumes. I had no way of getting down there in time to retrieve them so they would disappear. When I was sick as a kid and stayed home from school, I would read all day long. Since I wasn't permitted to watch TV, I would even read the encyclopedia, whatever I could get my hands on. My dad tried to explain that the house had become too big for him. Maybe he still had a mortgage to deal with or maybe he simply wanted to cash out. "I'm having a garage sale and everything must go," he said, but before hanging up he rather casually added, "Oh . . . and your Uncle Tony is dead."

"What?" I screamed. "What the hell happened?" My father in a monotone voice told me that my uncle had gotten up one morning, took out his hunting rifle, a double-barrel shotgun, went out to the backyard, sat down under the pear tree and blew his head off.

Aside from his duties at the hatchery, Uncle Tony grew Zoysia Grass. He covered his little quarter acre with it. The grass would eventually spread and become a perfect lawn. His yard looked like a golf course. I always wondered if he grew it just to show off his beloved pear tree. I wasn't surprised that he had gone to the pear tree that was so perfectly centered in his lovely lawn to end his life.

The news of his death was simply beyond belief. I felt my body go completely numb. What was wrong with my father? What happened to his heart? Did he even have one? Why was any of this normal behavior? No, most American families don't treat you like shit at a funeral and a few months later wrap a baseball bat around your head with the grizzly news of a dearly departed. This couldn't be perfectly normal.

I had to get myself back down to South Jersey to see Aunt Marie. When I walked in the back door she was sitting at the kitchen table where she always sat, with her elbows resting on that same tattered, cigarette burned, yellow plastic tablecloth. She looked up and glared at me. "Where have *you* been?" she demanded. I was still lost in confusion and asked her when this happened. "Three months ago!" she shouted at me. Decked out in denim from head to toe, I just stood there and began to cry, then I took a seat at the table right next to her and tried to give her a hug. She resisted. "I just found out yesterday," I said with my face covered in tears, "my father just called me yesterday!"

"That louse!" she said in half a voice. "You know I never liked that man." We both sat there crying and hugging each other. I asked her if I could stay for a day or two, and she quickly agreed. Marie had always been my champion; now it was time for me to be hers. As we talked I asked her to fill in some of the blanks for me. "How did my mother actually die? No one had ever told me."

Her answer was simple enough. With a face so drawn and exhausted she looked over at me and murmured, "Her heart burst. It just exploded and that was it." So had all those years of amphetamines and barbiturates actually caused her heart to literally explode? It still wasn't clear to me. Later of course, I would come to understand that she simply suffered a sudden and massive heart attack. Then I asked about Uncle Tony and she told me that he had gotten progressively worse, wasn't able to wash himself and depended on her for just about everything. "He was such a proud man, Gary, he just couldn't bear being reduced to an invalid," she said, tears streaming down her face. "I woke up that morning thinking that I'd heard a firecracker, and when I went to the back door I found him under the pear tree. There was blood everywhere. He had shot his head clean off. Oh, Gary, it was awful." I looked out the back door at the pear tree, remembering all the yellow jackets swarming around it in the summertime. I couldn't even bring myself to imagine the gory image that she had found. Imagine losing someone in such a way. I did my best to comfort her for a day or two, but I had to get back to the city. I gave her a big hug and kiss and said goodbye, promising to come back down for a weekend as soon as I could. She really needed me now. Even with all that I was trying to accomplish for myself, my aspirations, my music, there was no way that I could let her down. She needed me to be in it for the long run.

Back in New York, I sat staring blankly at my falafel sandwich, pondering what I was about to do. The Olive Tree on MacDougal Street had some of the best Middle Eastern food on the block. It was also the perfect place to hang out and wait your turn to perform your fifteen minutes of fame at the Gaslight, a music venue just across the street. I needed to put together a short "set list" of songs. I had signed up for "Hoot" night, now better known as "Open Mic" night but basically the same thing. This would be my first time performing in New York. Arriving a bit late, I managed to pull number eleven. So, in other words, I would be the eleventh performer that night, almost dead last.

Sam Hood, a local impresario, managed the Gaslight which was owned by his father, Clarence. It was every bit of an underground Greenwich Village hot spot plus it had serious history. Dylan had debuted "A Hard Rain's A-Gonna Fall" there. In fact the entire "Bleecker/MacDougal" area of the West Village had serious history. The Bitter End on Bleecker Street boasted the likes of Phil Ochs, Tim Hardin, Tom Paxton, Peter Paul and Mary, and of course Bob Dylan. The Cafe Wha? on MacDougal right across the street from the Gaslight was practically a residence to a young Jimi Hendrix as well as a regular hang for Dylan, Ginsberg, and a host of others. The whole of Greenwich Village reeked of musical history.

Making my way through the dimly lit room I grabbed a seat in the back. The act on stage called themselves "Laurel Canyon." They were a three girl folk group. Two of them played guitars and their harmonies were spot-on. The girl in the middle who sang had an exotic look about her. She was very thin with long, wispy, wavy brown hair, maybe not the prettiest girl in the world in the classic sense but she had a look that was intriguing and magnetic.

Frankly I don't remember all that much about my own performance. What I am able to conjure up was that I seemed to go into a trancelike state. I remember the lights shining on me and the blackness that was the audience, a decent amount of applause but not much more than that. I very quickly packed my guitar and left the stage heading for the street. As I was making my way to the door someone tapped my left shoulder. It was that singer from the "girl group." She stopped me and told me how much she liked my songs. She said, "They're better than what we usually get in here . . . My name is Dory." I introduced myself and after recovering from brief shock asked her if she would like to get some coffee. "Sure . . . I know this place called the Olive Tree," she said. "It's right across the street." She seemed to want to know everything about me. No member of the female persuasion had ever been quite so curious about me. None of my past girlfriends were ever as probing as this girl was. She told me that she lived in Brooklyn and that sometime I should come out there and hang with her and her friends as well as meet her brother Alan.

Alan Miles was in fact a staff songwriter for April-Blackwood, which was the publishing arm for CBS/Columbia. She seemed to think that he should hear my songs. Somehow I got up the nerve to invite her to visit me way uptown for an afternoon in Riverside Park and maybe some local food.

She said, "What about this Saturday?"

"Great!" I said, not missing a beat.

So when Saturday rolled around I had agreed to meet her at my subway stop at around 1:00 PM. I lived in a rough neighborhood and I definitely didn't want her roaming around. She finally got there, her hair even more dramatic than I remembered, appearing very waiflike in her suede vest and blue jean bell-bottoms. I offered to show her where I lived and maybe listen to some music together for a bit.

I put Cat Stevens' *Tea for the Tillerman* on the stereo and we just talked for a while. She had started to say something else when she stopped in mid-sentence and just looked at me. Then she said something really strange. "When I look at you and you seem so young and then I look again and you seem so old . . . it's really weird." That comment freaked me out a bit. In a strange way I understood what she was trying to say. I felt the same thing, kind of like a time shift but it left me unsettled. I think that perhaps my upbringing, all that early trauma, made me appear more mature, giving me the appearance of an old soul. I quickly changed the subject and suggested that we take a walk through Riverside Park just below my apartment building. We walked and joked around for some time until we had actually walked so far that we wound up almost a mile north at the little lighthouse under the George Washington Bridge. This was kind of a cool secret place right on the Hudson. We sat down and talked for a bit more and just stared at the river. Later we wound up back near my place at El Camaguey, a local Cuban diner right by the subway stop. Shredded beef and peas was my favorite dish. We had a late lunch, some café con leche and hugged goodbye, saying that we would see each other soon.

She called me the very next night saying that she had already talked to her brother and he really wanted to meet me.

"Well she probably hammered away at him until he caved in," I thought.

She said that I could go up to his office on my lunch break, and she would meet me there and introduce me to Alan. Apparently, his office was right around the corner from the record store where I worked. So armed with a couple of joints of my finest weed just in case the opportunity to be cordial presented itself, I made my way up to his office. I left my guitar at home that day as I intended to play a couple of new songs on piano that I had just written. Dory introduced me to Alan, who was nice enough, and also to his writing partner, a guy who went by the name of Troy . . . no last name, just Troy. Troy was a bit stocky in stature and I assumed that he had adopted the pseudonym as a sort of metaphor evoking an image of Homer's epic work. Now the four of us crammed into a tiny office with no windows and, for mood, a desk lamp with a blue bulb. I lit a joint, passed it, and sat down at their upright piano.

I started with a song that I had just written simply entitled "Lately." It was a ballad about love lost, people growing apart, that sort of thing. When I finished, I could barely see the smiles on their faces through the billows of smoke. "That was incredible!" Alan said. Troy and Dory agreed. I didn't want to press my luck but just the same I tried one more song called "Cobblestones and Carriages." Even though I might have been channeling Elton John who had recently burst upon the scene, this was not a straight ahead love song. The lyrics were kind of spacey and mystical, much more poetic and out there. "I was always on the inside . . . You were quite misunderstood, but when it came down to finding out who was to blame . . . Well the Cobblestones' grey and the Carriage is pulling away." They went nuts. Alan lunged forward as though he forgot the desk was there. Troy, who was the lyricist for the writing team stood up and said, "Man! I have NEVER heard anything like that before!" I had to get back to the store so I got up, thanked them all, gave Dory a kiss on the cheek, and said goodbye. As I was leaving, Alan said, "Hey Gary, you're welcome back anytime!"

"Great," I said fading into the hall, "and thanks, I'll take you up on that!" So with that it was back to Nappy's.

I thought to myself that maybe all my time spent reading poets like E. E. Cummings and T. S. Eliot had actually paid off. I was writing songs that people thought sounded pretty cool but no one understood a single word of. I think that I was simply painting with words. Dylan seemed to be experimenting with that kind of thing and I couldn't resist trying to emulate his genius.

I was making a decent wage at the record store and with my rent so reasonable I had some extra cash to burn. I would usually spend it on the finest drugs I could find, mostly weed but I was always looking for fine hashish as well. I loved that soft black hash with the white line running through it, the opiated kind. Showing up at Alan and Troy's office for lunch became a regular thing. Sometimes we actually ate lunch and sometimes I would bring my guitar in and try out other songs on them, and of course, there were always what Troy referred to as my "softballs" of hash. I was starting to wonder if these guys just liked me because I would show up a couple of days a week and get them high. Just when I was beginning to think that Alan and Troy might be a dead end for me, the door of their dimly blue-lit cubicle opened and in walked Joel Diamond with a strange looking guy. Joel ran April-Blackwood and introduced his thin, long-haired friend as Al. He asked Al to sit down and play us a tune that he had just finished. Without saying a word the guy took over the piano and played "I Can't Quit Her." After the very last note, we all said a collective, "Holy shit!" Al Kooper, who had already had some success with The Blues Project, went on to put together one of the greatest American bands of all time, Blood Sweat & Tears. I decided to keep hanging out.

Another afternoon in the cubicle of blue light, Alan turned to me saying, "You know man, we've been talking and we really want to help you somehow. You're good . . . really good. We're gonna make some phone calls, maybe we can get you some kind of audition, get you a job in the business." I assumed that what he meant was that they would try to hook me up with a writer's gig at a music publisher.

The very next time I showed up for lunch at their office I met their friend Ray Wexler. He wore a jacket and dress shirt with nice slacks; we were always in jeans. Ray worked for E. H. Morris, which was a publisher that I had never heard of, but what the hell, I played him some of the songs that I had first played for Alan and Troy. He then asked me to come to his office and play for his boss, Agnes Kelliher. I was now losing it. This was righteously crazy. This kind of "audition" for a publisher was very specific to that era. At that time a publisher would sign you because they believed in your talent, your potential. Unfortunately, those days are long gone, and today you have to walk in the door with something already happening, a bubbling hit in your hip pocket.

E. H. Morris was mainly a theatre publisher that owned the rights to shows like *Hello Dolly, Mame, Bye Bye Birdie*, and a ton of other Broadway hits. In the world of musical theatre this company was at the top of the heap. What puzzled me was that I was writing anything but theatre.

Their offices were in a beautiful private town house over near Sixth Avenue, east of where I worked. That was the area of town where all the "big" companies had their offices.

After work, at the appointed time I went over to meet with Ray and Agnes. Her office had a large private office on the first floor which looked like a formal living room complete with long couches, coffee table, art on the walls, and a lovely Steinway grand piano. Agnes, who preferred to be called "Aggie," was larger than life, a tall and beautiful older woman with perfect blonde hair and impeccably dressed. She smelled of money. She was the general manager of the company and answered directly to E. H. "Buddy" Morris. The enigmatic Mr. Morris I had yet to meet. He lived in Palm Springs but kept an apartment at the St. Regis Hotel nearby. Morris had put the power to sign someone into Aggie's hands.

I played those same first couple of songs for her and Ray. I noticed that Aggie had cracked a slight smile; she seemed to be intrigued. Ray looked over at her with a facial expression that seemed to say, "You see? Didn't I tell you?"

Aggie then asked me to wait outside so she and Ray could have a word. I sat waiting by the reception desk staring at the works of Jasper Johns and Jackson Pollack. I stared at them just long enough to realize that these were not prints. These paintings were originals. About ten minutes later Ray poked his head out and asked me to come back in. Aggie sat quietly on the couch just smiling as she let Ray do the talking. Ray asked me if I wanted to sign with them as a staff writer for $50 a week. I didn't even think about it, I just spouted out "Yes!"

"Now you understand," he went on, "that the company will own everything that you write, but we're willing to pay you to simply write songs." I said that would be just fine and thanked them both profusely. Ray said that he could have a contract ready by the beginning of the following week. I could sign and start right away.

I also had just realized that this was the second person named "Aggie" in my life. How could I know at the time that she would also become a "director," so to speak? Things were simply connecting, feeling like fate. I had been in New York only nine months and I was signed by a major publisher.

I didn't know what to do. Should I call someone? If so, who? At a time like this it would be normal to call home, but I felt estranged from my father. Just the same I couldn't see straight. On the train ride home that night I wondered how I should break the news to my boss at the record store. Someone else might have tried to hold on to that job, be practical and wait out the future. But as "The Fool" card is depicted in the tarot deck, I was gleefully walking off a cliff.

The next morning I went to work with some degree of trepidation. I had become something of a valued employee and I had to tell Max Roth, the gruff manager of the record store, that Friday would be my last day. He was not pleased. In fact, he actually sulked most of that morning. Then around 12:30, he asked me to go out and get his lunch for him as I would every day. He always ate the same thing, boneless-skinless imported sardines with lettuce, tomato, and mayonnaise and a slice of onion on a Kaiser roll.

This time when I returned with it, he took the bag from me and kind of gave me a wink. He was silently wishing me well. Almost everyone who worked at Colony was a wannabe or a has-been. Very few trains ever left that station, but I was moving on.

At moments like these I would mentally wander off and wonder about my real mother and if she might just be wondering about me. Would she be proud of what I had become?

The thought of finding her never really left my mind. It may not have always been at the forefront but still always there, following me as if my own shadow.

CHAPTER 8

SWEET BEGINNINGS

A side from the lovely office that Aggie occupied on the first floor of the E. H. Morris town house, there was a wide curving stairway that led to the second floor. There were two large offices each with a piano, as well as stereo equipment including a turntable and a reel-to-reel tape machine. In those days they were the state of the art tools of the trade. Ray Wexler, the guy largely responsible for signing me, occupied the back office. This room offered a long leather couch and a deep pile carpet. On his office wall hung a few pieces of framed sheet music. I remember seeing "Autumn Leaves" and "Stormy Weather" hanging there. These were just two among many of the classic standards that the company owned. The front office facing the street was not so luxurious and was up for grabs to whomever wanted to use it to write. The third floor housed the famed theatre department. Morris didn't have many rock/pop writers; in fact I was one of two. The other was Ginger Greco who just happened to be married to Ray. Ginger was pretty, looked kind of European, very thin with wavy dark hair, and a great sense of humor. She and I got

along right off even though I was the new kid. Much more sea-
soned than I, she would often give me constructive criticism
when I would play something for her that I was working on.
After knowing me for only a short time, Ginger walked in one
day and said she had a surprise for me. She handed me a grey
hard-shell guitar case saying, "This is for you." I opened it
and nearly passed out. It was a vintage Martin acoustic guitar,
the 000-18 model, probably worth thousands. I hugged her so
hard, thanking her over and over, and we both started to cry a
bit. "Thank you, thank you," I said hugging her tightly. "This
is just . . . thank you!" It was such a great moment with another songwriter. Maybe it also meant that she saw something
special in me that I wasn't quite able to clearly see just yet.

When I had completed something new, the first order of business was to play it for Aggie. She and I were warming up to
each other as well. Here was this dynamic, almost shark of
a woman who also seemed to have a sweet and naive side to
her. Behind all her hardened business savvy facade, she was a
softhearted, good Irish Catholic girl from Queens. One day I
was running a song by her that I just finished when she tilted
her head to one side and said,
    "You know, you should demo that song."
    "You mean in a recording studio?" I asked.
    "Why yes, of course. I'll make the arrangements."
    She had Ray put together a rhythm section for me. The
bass player, Jim Gregory, had been a longtime session player,
and his friend Gregg Diamond had worked with a number of
bands and was quite the socialite, always making an appearance wherever the action was. Gregg was one of the sons of
the "Diamond Family," and by that I mean Diamond Walnuts,
Diamond Matches, Diamond Salt, Diamond everything. He was

flamboyant, wore makeup and sometimes a scarf and top hat, and the coolest clothes. He always looked like he had just returned from a shopping spree in London. Whatever clothes you saw on the emerging rock stars of the day, Gregg was already wearing them. I had also become something of a clotheshorse by that time, wearing brightly colored "stovepipe" corduroy pants and platform boots. It was the "Glitter/Glam" seventies, androgyny was the order of the day, and David Bowie was at the forefront of that scene.

The seventies was a great time for the music business. Artists of all kinds were getting signed, especially singer/songwriters. Even publishers like E. H. Morris were trying to turn out artists. It wasn't only about the money; there was a prestige aspect that had become so very valuable. A company like Morris had the potential to "cross over" from being just a theatre publisher to actually competing in the Top 40 and rock arenas, broadening their viability.

The studio was ODO on 54th Street. As the industry's audio recording standard had evolved to sixteen tracks, soon to be twenty-four, ODO had become mostly known as a "demo" studio. It was a very nice 8-track studio, complete with drums, amps, a Baldwin grand piano, and even a harpsichord. We had no rehearsal at all, I simply taught the song to them in the studio. These musicians were pros and picked up on what I was doing right away. When it came time to "roll tape" it all came together in only two or three takes.

A day or two had passed when Ray Wexler cornered me, wanting to talk in private. "Come in my office and have a seat," he said, heading for the chair behind the desk. Folding his hands and laying his elbows on his desk he leaned forward. "You know, I think of you as being more than just a songwriter," he said, looking me straight in the eye. "I think that with my help you could actually take a stab at the big time."

"Wow, that's great!" I said, "I'm really flattered." All of this was going really fast. I needed to take a breath. "Can I have some time to think about it?" I asked. "Sure! Take all the time you need," he said, stretching his arms out wide. So I breathed for about a day and then told Ray that I would sign on. Ray Wexler was a hustler, a carnival sideshow barker. He was loud, brash, and terribly overweight, everything you could ever dream of in a personal manager.

Within a week Ray and I were sitting across the desk from Jerry Love, the head of A&R for Motown's satellite office in New York. I got the impression that Ray already knew Jerry well enough to be able to just walk me in. Oddly enough, my old "Famly Syrkle" drummer, Arthur's cousin Alan, whose name I dropped to get the gig at Colony, had at one time worked for Jerry Love. I never saw a contract or met with an attorney, which I later discovered would have been standard protocol, but suddenly I, still very much a neophyte, was now "signed" to Motown. It was described to me as a developmental deal, which meant they would put together a modest budget for studio time and I was to make a three or four song demo to officially present to the record company before actually doing an entire record. The studio was the fabled Record Plant. We would be working in studio B, the same room where Jimi Hendrix recorded "Electric Ladyland." We would be working with an up-and-coming engineer, Jay Messina. Jay had already worked with Miles Davis and would go on to work with John Lennon, Aerosmith, and Cheap Trick among countless others.

With the same band as before, Jim Gregory on bass and Gregg Diamond on drums, we set about to cut four tunes. Jay Messina, an incredibly skilled audio engineer, was making everything sound crystal clear and just perfect. This project would turn out to be better than imagined. The sound of the recordings as well as the songs chosen all blended together into some kind of gestalt of Elton John, Crosby, Stills & Nash, David Bowie, and The Beatles. I was channeling everybody. Finally I had a four song "artist demo" that was to be submitted to Jerry Love for Motown. I think that, with the exception of Rare Earth, who just had the hits, "Get Ready" and "Celebrate," I just might have been the only other white artist ever signed to this classic label. At the time I didn't care what label I was signed to, I just wanted to make a record.

I checked in with Ray nearly every day to see if there might be a positive word from Mr. Love. Ray began to avoid me. Then, without warning I hit my first major obstacle. The four-song demo would never even be heard. Just like that, I no longer had a relationship with Motown, and as it turned out whatever advance the label gave me was pocketed by Ray, and the musicians and studio were not paid. There was no approval, no money, and no deal. Ray Wexler, as I eventually discovered from others on the office staff, had a personal gambling problem. Apparently, it was common knowledge, although I think that everyone at Morris had kept it from Aggie. I can't believe that she would have just allowed all this to happen to me. She couldn't have known.

"Oh, well that's just fucking great!" I thought. Echoes of John Mahoney's "You'll never amount to anything" from graduation day repeated in my head. Ray disappeared from Morris immediately, although his wife, Ginger, remained. I soon learned that they were headed for divorce.

All during this time those songwriter "hangs" had expanded beyond lunch. Now they seemed to be happening more and more at the Morris town house after business hours. Since Ray's departure we had commandeered his old office. Alan and Troy from April-Blackwood would come by and bring some friends, like Scott English who had written a song entitled "Brandy." Scott had also written "Bend Me Shape Me" which was a hit for The American Breed. He would always bring along a reel-to-reel tape that just had the music to "Brandy" without vocals. Scott had actually had a hit as an artist with this song in the UK, so he would stand up and sing the lead. I would struggle to describe his singing voice, but in a way I suppose that he was the perfect example of why some songwriters don't always become pop stars. He sounded a bit like an elf on helium. I guess the UK was cool with that but we would all have a giggle. Deep down we knew that "Brandy" would someday become a huge hit. As a side note, most of us know that song today as "Mandy." Clive Davis, then president of Columbia records, who eventually left the company after being accused of embezzling funds to pay for his son's Bar Mitzvah, would become the head of his own record label named Arista records. After signing Manilow he insisted the song title be changed before its release as to not have it confused with "Brandy (You're a Fine Girl)" which had become a hit by the band Looking Glass.

One night Ginger showed up with Stan Vincent who had written "O-o-H Child" recorded by the Five Stairsteps. There were others who drifted in and out, one of them being Richard Porterfield who worked for Atlantic records, always bringing along his friend Jeremy, an aspiring songwriter. We would haul in sandwiches and beer and I always supplied the weed.

Everyone would take turns swapping songs, getting high, laughing, and carrying on until about 9:00 PM when the janitor locked the town house door for the night. Sometimes after

the nine o'clock curfew some of us would break off into smaller groups and find another place to commiserate. One night
after a long absence, Richard Porterfield showed up but this
time without Jeremy. Alan called across the room, "Hey Rich,
where's Jeremy?" Richard hung his head for a moment, then
looked up and quite soberly said, "Jeremy's dead."

"What?" we all gasped. He went on to explain that Jeremy
had been suffering from a serious drug problem mostly with
"downs" and had overdosed on Quaaludes. So that was it, or so
we thought. This shy and nice enough guy who always hung
with Richard was now dead. We were all pretty upset. Even
though deaths from Quaalude overdose were becoming increasingly more common, it just didn't easily sink in; for some
reason, it didn't seem real. What we didn't know at the time
was that Richard and Jeremy were actually lovers who both
wished to remain in the closet. Richard was lying to us about
Jeremy's death and had in fact simply cut him loose, although
at the moment, all that remained a secret.

Just the same, Jeremy's alleged Quaalude overdose got me
thinking about that very first day at Catholic school with my
mother stuffing my mouth full of aspirin. She had taught me a
golden lesson in masking pain, both physical and emotional, a
lesson that I would find difficult to unlearn as I would eventually find myself caught somewhere between shadow and light.
I recalled the times that I would call home before my mother
passed. I would always be able to tell if she was speeding or just
totally downed out.

The only thing constant is change, and one afternoon Aggie
announced that Mr. Morris had decided to sell the town house.
His plan was to relocate the offices to a new high-rise at 56th
Street and Avenue of the Americas that was just opening its
doors. The office setup would be somewhat similar to that of

the town house, only now E. H. Morris was sharing an entire floor of a giant skyscraper with just one other much smaller company. There was a large living room that would have southern and western exposures housing the Steinway Grand, Aggie's office just adjacent the big room, which was also kind of like a living room, just a bit cozier than her former office. She even had her own private bathroom built in across the hall from her office. There were several smaller offices that would serve as writers' rooms, with everyone, including the theatre and accounting department, all on one floor in one gigantic suite.

A couple of new writers were brought on board as well. Hayden Wayne, who was a Juilliard graduate and much more of a theatrical/classical writer, was one. A few months later another writer named Thom Fallick joined us, brought in by a new talent scout. Thom was doing more of a "Dylan meets Jim Croce" kind of thing. He played acoustic twelve-string and wrote some pretty good songs. He eventually changed his name to Thom Kidrin for somewhat obvious reasons. Thom and I became friendly and would hang out together at night sometimes or on a weekend. Aside from having a great place to hang out and work on my material, I had also gained some new friends in Thom and Hayden. Ginger, who may have felt challenged by these new artistic arrivals was now asserting her presence and becoming quite the "Queen Bee."

Sometimes I would take up residence in Aggie's office. She didn't seem to mind; in fact I think that she liked having me around. Agnes never really moved that far from home. She was a girl who married young, lived in Jackson Heights, a nice neighborhood in Queens, and never had children. One afternoon I thought to tell her about my adoption status and the inner feelings that my mother was still alive. I sensed that she might be receptive to my plight and maybe have some words of wisdom. We sat side by side on her cushy couch as I laid out some of my personal past to her. She seemed to be touched by the story and promised me that she would put together a list of agencies that helped adoptees try to find their families. It would be my very first practical step in the process of trying to find my birthmother.

One afternoon, Aggie was having a meeting with Ginger in her office with the doors closed. "What's this?" I wondered. Eventually Aggie called me into the meeting. "I would like to put a band together behind Ginger and her music," Aggie explained, "and I would like for you to be a part of it . . . what do you think?"

"That sounds great!" I said. "So who else is involved?" Aggie went on that she was thinking that Hayden, one of the new writers, would play keyboards and we would get back Jim Gregory and Gregg Diamond to be the rhythm section. I jumped in and enthusiastically added, "And I have a name for the band . . . Sweet Beginnings!" It was really just a reversal of the "Bitter End," the famous folk venue on Bleecker Street, but Aggie seemed to like it. Thinking back, it was a pretty lame suggestion. This prospective project would be E. H. Morris's first attempt to cross over into pop territory.

During this time I had begun the slow and tedious process of changing my name. Not legally, but with some formality. I had always remembered something that my mother had told me years before when I questioned her about my adoption. After telling me that my real mom had died giving birth, she added a few more words that were possibly intended to soften the blow. She told me that my mom looked just like me, red hair and freckles, and that in a handwritten note that my birth-mother asked to be passed along by her caseworker to the prospective adoptive mother, she very politely asked that my name be "David." It never occurred to me to ask how she knew what my real mother looked like, especially if she had died during childbirth. My mother actually tried to honor that request in her own way. She made David my middle name, naming me Gary David Mesiano. She said that she picked the name Gary because she didn't want other people to shorten my name when they addressed me. That kind of thing is so commonly done. You call David, Dave . . . or Charles, Chuck, so for some reason, in her mind there wasn't any way to shorten the name Gary. Naturally the first thing everyone did was call me "Gar." Now my next problem was trying to get everyone that I had already met in New York to start calling me David. Not easy.

Still breaking in my new persona as David, we set about to put the band together by rehearsing at Baggie's, a popular space located way downtown on Grand Street. They had three rehearsal rooms at Baggie's, but Agnes always went top notch so we took over the "Showcase" room. It had a very nice stage, a great sound system, professional lighting, and a whole lot of space, some of which was taken up by rows of folding chairs that could accommodate a small audience. Everyone who was anyone rehearsed at Baggie's. It was without a doubt the hippest rehearsal space in all of Manhattan, located in what would eventually become Soho, long before anyone had ever thought to conjoin the phrase "South of Houston."

This was a great opportunity for me not only because Aggie was serious and had the power to make things happen, but also because I now had an excuse to buy myself a proper electric guitar and learn how to play lead. I went to 48th Street, which at the time was music row, with store after store full of musical instruments. I bought myself a 1967 Fender Stratocaster, the same kind of guitar used by Jimi Hendrix. This was way beyond cool. This was the guitar that I had always wanted since first seeing Jimi on TV. Down at Baggie's we were knee-deep in rehearsal. We had all pretty much decided that this would be a six song showcase. That might be a tall order but we could always cut a song or two at the last minute.

When we finally had our presentation together, Aggie wanted to come and see a "dry run." I don't think that Agnes had ever been below 42nd Street. The idea of going to somewhere that was even farther south than Greenwich Village was kind of a big deal for her. Naturally she took a cab. When she arrived her perfume filled the room, and she was wearing one of her "ready for business" pantsuits, a very slim, tailored, turquoise outfit. She took a seat in the first row. Ginger's songs were what would have been described in that day as typical "Chick Rock." A song that particularly struck me seemed to portray her inner fear of men. She called it "Fag Hag." We performed, not just playing and singing, but "performed" our entire set for her. By that I mean that we all imagined that we were in Madison Square Garden in front of thousands of adoring fans.

At the end of our last song, we thanked the invisible audience and left the stage to huddle together in the corner of the room. "Clap . . . Clap . . . Clap," we heard coming from her hands.

Oh no, was that good or bad? She asked us to assemble and told us that she was going to make "a call." The next day at Morris, she told us all that we would be doing a showcase for a special person. After pressing her for this person's identity she finally told us that John Hammond Sr. had agreed to come to Baggie's and have a look.

John Hammond was the "uncrowned King of the Music Business." He was one of the most influential people of twentieth-century popular music. As a talent scout for Columbia records he was responsible for discovering and signing the greats from Benny Goodman to Bob Dylan and eventually, Bruce Springsteen. Although a member of the Vanderbilt family, he had a reputation for being very down to earth. There was nothing flamboyant about his appearance. He wore a well-tailored suit and tie, his haircut was short military style, and though quite wealthy, he took the subway. He was unassuming, tall, thin, and all business. He was also known to actually have "ears," a term still used today to describe anyone in the record industry who can recognize real talent. I had heard the story of "Hammond's Folly." Mitch Miller, who later had the musical variety show on TV called *Sing Along With Mitch* was working as a talent scout at Columbia records alongside a young John Hammond. Hammond had stumbled across this kid named Zimmerman down in the Village and one day convinced Miller to accompany him downtown to hear the guy perform. Miller walked away with Hammond saying, "Sorry John . . . I just don't get it!" Hammond then signed Robert Zimmerman a/k/a Bob Dylan to Columbia. Since Dylan's first few releases were recorded "live to tape" without any outside accompaniment, these early recordings cost almost nothing to produce. Initially, they didn't sell very well and the whole project became known as "Hammond's Folly." Of course Mr. Hammond did manage to have the last laugh.

Now this living legend was coming downtown to see us. What would be our "big chance" just got very real. We all got chills. He took a seat in the center of the front row, pulled a memo book and a pen from his jacket pocket, and waited for us to begin. Once more, we performed our set like we were in front of a huge audience. Looking back, I think that we may have nervously cut the set short because we didn't want to take up so much of his valuable time. At the conclusion he nodded his head, thanked everyone very sincerely, shook Aggie's hand,

and slipped away. Aggie then looked at us and said, "Sorry everybody, but I think that was a 'pass.'" Okay, not great but oh the thrill of it all. At least I could breathe again.

CHAPTER 9

JUSTICE

The next day I went over to April-Blackwood to see Alan and Troy. I was in the middle of telling them what had happened at Baggie's when Alan put his finger to his mouth indicating that I be quiet. "Troy and I just got fired. Friday is our last day," he solemnly said. I couldn't believe it. Alan was planning to move to L.A. and try his hand out there. "Troy," I said, "what about you?" He slumped down in the chair and rested his arms on his thighs. Wiping his tears away with the sleeve of his camouflage fatigue jacket he slurred, "I just don't know what I'm going to do . . . I really don't have any place to go. I'm broke or I would go to L.A. too."

"All right, hang on," I said. "Let me see if I can come up with something and I'll call you tomorrow." "Fine," he mumbled, hanging his head even a bit more. I wasn't absolutely sure whether or not Troy was truly upset or just milking the moment.

I ran back to the Morris office and cornered Aggie to suggest that she bring Troy on board. "Well our roster is full right now," she insisted.

"I understand, but you really have to see just how talented this guy is before you pass on him," I said with all the conviction that I could summon. Troy was not only a gifted lyricist but he was a fantastic singer. His voice had power, and he was quite the showman. At our songwriter "hangs" when Troy got up to sing, he would stop the room as he channeled his idol Elvis Presley.

Aggie finally agreed to have him come over and "audition." I called him and told him to be there at one o'clock the next day and to not wear his usual camouflage fatigues or anything shabby but to look nice and respectable. Troy didn't play guitar all that well, just enough to accompany himself. He appeared at the appointed time, and we sat together in Aggie's office. I loaned him my guitar, the Martin that Ginger had given me, and he played and sang a ballad that was all over the radio, "Me and Bobby McGee." About halfway through, Agnes glanced over at me offering a tiny grin. He killed it.

Laying the guitar against the couch, Troy left the room for a moment. Aggie turned to me and asked, "But can he write?"

"Yes he can write, he's a great lyricist, and I apologize for him not being fully prepared," I said. Back from the men's room I asked Troy, "Why didn't you bring demos of the songs that you wrote with Alan?!"

"Sorry man, I was in such a hurry to be on time that I forgot," he said looking down. I was visibly upset having gone out on a limb for him. Turning to Agnes I promised that he would bring them in for her to hear and that I would be more than willing to try to cowrite with him myself. This is something that I had never done. I had never cowritten a song with any-one except for my quirky piano teacher Mr. Thompson, when I was nine. I might be promising her more than I could deliver, but he and Alan had done so much for me, I felt I had to do something. After hearing Troy's demos, Aggie gave her con-sent. Troy had a job, and I was his new cowriter. For me these were uncharted waters, but I honestly wanted it all to work out for the best. Surprisingly, the first time that we sat down to write together it was almost magical. He was the "down-to-earth" lyrical guy and I was the "ethereal" lyrical guy. One great example of this was a song called "Corrina Cheevers." Troy came up with the title and a story line about an under-age madam who ran a brothel down south. "Corrina Cheevers your house has a name," he wrote. "Distant believers all visit the same," I answered. Then the chorus exploded with, "Like an unforgotten ending, you are the song I'm sending . . . Lis-ten for the music starting to play . . . Oh like a Sunday martyr down where the willows holler, drinking from the river that took you away." Troy had a great sense of melody and would pick up the guitar or sit at the piano and say something like, "I'm hearing something like this." And nine times out of ten he was right. We were a great team, and we began churning them out, song after song.

We would be writing up-tempo rock songs and then turn around and come up with an incredibly sweet ballad. I was becoming a better writer because of the collaboration. One of the best things about hanging out with Troy was our shared sense of humor. We could make each other laugh, and I mean "belly laugh," when you hold your stomach, roll off the couch onto the floor, and suddenly find yourself at serious risk of losing your lunch. We had become not only a powerful song-writing team but also good friends. Within no time, Troy and

I had written enough songs for more than one record, probably enough for two. It was time to get Aggie's attention and get her to sit down and listen to some of it.

We had our act down. I would accompany on either guitar or piano, Troy would sing lead and I would provide the harmonies. His voice was gritty, mine was sweet, and at the time, I was able to hit some of the really high notes while still remaining in "full voice" and not defaulting to "falsetto," which was the vocal range that Frankie Valli and The Four Seasons had made so popular. I came up with the band name "Justice" and we both agreed, that's what we would call ourselves.

After playing our stuff for Aggie we could almost see her brain at work just by the look on her face. Naturally she really liked the songs, but there was more to it than that. She finally had the act she was looking for. She looked at us with a very serious face and said, "You boys are going to need a record deal," and then said that she would make a few calls. Enter Sandy Yaguda, who was once a member of Jay and The Americans, and had become the head of A&R for ABC/Dunhill in New York. This was the label that signed the Mamas and the Papas and The Grassroots.

Sandy really liked our stuff and suggested that we do some demos with him as producer to present to the label. There was some initial discussion of money. I seem to remember Sandy promising us fifteen hundred bucks as an initial "pocket money" advance. That was a lot of money for us in those days. We had assembled a few musicians, bass player and drummer, and headed back to ODO studios to make the demo for ABC/Dunhill. Troy was always short on money and consequently, he made cash his primary focus. I just wanted to concentrate on the music. When Troy heard that the check Sandy promised would be delayed, he freaked. Ripping off his headphones and throwing them to the floor he walked up to the control room window and started yelling at the glass. "Hey man! What the fuck?! I mean what the fuck?" He began making all kinds of bodily gyrations looking like a rogue gorilla aiming his wrath directly at Sandy. I put my guitar down, walked up behind him, and punched him in the back of the head, yelling, "What the fuck is wrong with you, man?" Troy turned around and punched me in the chest, and the next thing I knew we were screaming and rolling on the studio floor trying to take a clean shot at each other. Through the control room window I saw the engineer jump out of his seat and the next moment Sandy rushed in to try and break it up. Troy eventually calmed down but I was really pissed. We reluctantly made up, recorded the demo, and waited to hear back from Sandy. Were we getting signed or not? Well apparently not, as Sandy called to inform us that ABC/Dunhill was in fact going under and that he was losing his job. Snuffed again. We may have just been knocked down but Justice would be done! A couple of days went by when Agnes asked us to be at her office at 1:00 PM for a meeting. "What's this about?" I asked. "I just want you boys to meet someone . . . who may be able to help," she said.

Troy and I arrived at Aggie's office on time. After a few minutes two men appeared at the door. Aggie beckoned them in, and we both stood up and shook their hands as they were introduced. "This is Bruce Henderson and David Levine," she firmly said, as if to cover just a hint of awkwardness about the moment. We hadn't heard of these guys and I was wondering if they had actually "shopped" themselves around town to some of the labels and publishers. Agnes took the ball and began to explain that Bruce and David were aspiring managers, and what they may lack in experience they gained in sheer drive.

Bruce seemed to be the alpha dog of the two; he also seemed to give the impression that his expertise was more on the creative side, while David came off as more of the business guy, but together they made a good presentation.

Bruce had money and a family estate up in Woodstock, New York. He suggested that if we were to get seriously involved that the two of us should start hanging out in Woodstock and maybe even rent an apartment or house where we could be out of the city and really concentrate on writing songs. It was my understanding that this would be a kind of "get to know us" working sabbatical. We would physically be in close proximity to Bruce, Aggie would be forwarding our weekly checks, and once some sense of bonding to Bruce and David had occurred we would probably return to the city. I never imagined that we would actually be living there for any length of time. Just the same, this was all sounding quite lovely and idyllic. Troy and I were preparing to pack. In fact, in my head, I was already there.

CHAPTER 10

WOODSTOCK

The leaves were just turning to a colorful spectacle in Woodstock, New York, which was still very much a hippie town. Troy, who was from rural Maryland and as a kid sang Presley songs at the local union hall, was not the hippie type, but I think that he was going to give it a go. That's where he and I differed. He was a good seven years older than me and brought up on Elvis. I was brought up on the Beatles. That's the element that made our writing relationship work so well, it juxtaposed us while at the same time cementing us together. We shared a symbiotic "odd couple" dynamic as well. I was "Felix". Settling in, we spent some time at Bruce's estate on Cooper's Lake Road. This lovely tree-lined road surrounded by woods, wrapped around Cooper's Lake which was part of the local reservoir system. His family had named the estate "Brigadoon" after the fabled town that appeared in Scotland every one hundred years or so.

The main house was very large, two stories and sprawling from within. There must have been at least six bedrooms plus a swimming pool and tennis court. Of course there was Bruce and his mother, Janet, a rather eccentric woman with flaming red hair, clearly a Katherine Hepburn type, her second husband, Walter, whose laugh resembled the quack of a duck, Bruce's German shepherd, "Bacchus," and a multitude of various other characters. At the far end of the house was the "nursery." There had been a very serious fire at the house many years earlier. As the story goes, an old man died trying to save his grandchildren who were trapped in that room. They all perished. Everyone would whisper about how the house was haunted. The ghost of the grandfather was said to appear at the basement door. He might even walk into the living room but not too far in. He wore work boots or rubbers.

I can swear to God that one afternoon as I was sitting in the living room reading a paper, with the TV volume on low, I heard someone come up the steps from the basement and then step into the living room. All the time I was flashing back to my childhood experiences on Roberts Boulevard in our redbrick house. I held that paper to my head, covering my face, but when I looked down I saw boots. Holy shit! This was for real!

I was shaking from just looking at this apparitional footwear. These were the galoshes of a ghost. Eventually, the moment passed as though it never was. Indeed it may have been all my imagination. I still can't be sure.

At Bruce's suggestion, Troy and I secured an apartment at Woodstock Estates. Woodstock Estates had a main house with some "alternative" housing that seemed to be built later on as rentals. Originally this was the home of Theodore Sturgeon, the science fiction/horror writer and director. Apparently, he had since removed himself from the picture and left this property to his estranged wife and very cute eighteen year old daughter. She was a very thin girl with a big ball of tight curly hair, who tossed me a fetching glance. The hamlet of Woodstock was originally established in 1903 as the Byrdcliff art colony. Having a population of no more than three thousand at the time, it was nestled in a beautiful mountainous area of Ulster County in upstate New York. Woodstock radiated from the town's center which was its village green. The famed Woodstock music festival actually occurred in Bethel, New York, a good hour and a half away. We settled into a small two bedroom apartment with a fireplace in the living area. It was tiny but good enough for us. We were able to use Bruce Henderson's account at Sam's Corner Market just up the road, so we lived primarily on ham and cheese sandwiches.

A few doors down from us lived a couple of aspiring songwriters, Sandy Zydel and her boyfriend. They had an act together and would occasionally perform in town at a local pub. I was really attracted to Sandy but alas she was taken. She in turn introduced me to her friend Laurie Harris who was a real beauty but she too was in a relationship. I was looking for love in apparently all the wrong places. Both Laurie and Sandy worked as assistants to Albert Grossman, who was probably best known for putting Peter, Paul and Mary together as well as being Bob Dylan's manager. His offices were in Bearsville, just outside of Woodstock proper.

Troy and I were driving a rental car that Bruce was paying for. Troy seemed to feel that our image had to be impeccable, so anytime we put a scratch or a dent in it we would simply drive to the rental place in Kingston and get another car. We had a different car just about every two weeks or so. The rumor mill was buzzing around town that we were drug dealers, as apparently the townspeople found the constant car switching to be somewhat suspicious. Troy often would wear a large blue denim hat with a big round brim and shiny metal studs, that would complete the image of his supposed nefarious character. In fact the hat used to belong to me but he begged me to give it to him.

We began to hang out in town at the Cafe Espresso, which was located right in the middle of town adjacent the village green. The girl working the bar was incredibly beautiful. She had long, flowing, wavy blonde hair and lush full lips. Troy was determined to get her into his corner. We would sit and drink, maybe play a few games of "Pong," the only video game around at that time, and Troy would try to work his charms. Eventually it happened and he and Alexandra became sort of an item. Alexandra lived with her friend Jessie Lee and I wound up with Jessie. She wasn't a classic beauty like Alexandra but she was nice enough to hang out with. At that point, I just needed sex. Badly.

Eventually Bruce Henderson had gotten tired of paying for the rental cars so we gathered some money together with Bruce's help and bought ourselves a used car. Not just any used car, this was a maroon 1965 Chevrolet Impala with black interior. Troy was now in his "driving glory" with his blue denim wide brim hat with all the studs making a serious fashion statement. One night I decided to take the car into town and hang with Jessie for a while. There was snow on the ground and the roads were icy. The driveway into Woodstock Estates was long, winding, and lined with trees that opened up to a clearing at its end. The main house was on the left and the smaller rental cottages were on the right. When I returned home and pulled in, I lost control of the car. I skidded from side to side managing to hit every single tree in the driveway like I was in a pinball machine. When I finally got to our apartment I walked around the car to have a look. It was dark but it appeared as though there might be several dents on both sides. So I just walked inside, threw the keys on the kitchen table, and called to Troy, "Hey man . . . I just wrecked the car . . . good night!" The next morning Troy inspected the damage. It wasn't really as bad as I had originally thought. He turned to me and said, "Look man, I'm just glad that you're all right."

Bruce and David were busy trying to get Justice a record deal. They approached Rick Marotta to produce the demos. Rick was one of the most popular studio drummers on the east coast, so he would be hiring Hugh McCracken to play guitar. Hugh had worked with artists ranging from Laura Nyro to B. B. King. Rick also slated the great Tony Levin to play bass. We were to record back in studio B at the Record Plant with Jay Messina at the board. I was very hopeful that this time around everything would run as smoothly as planned and the result would simply be nothing less than top shelf. Bruce had just recently rented an apartment in Greenwich Village at Number 48 Eighth Street, right behind Electric Lady studios. This garden apartment had a private entrance with a rock garden, bamboo trees, and a small man-made stream. The inside was painted purple and deep blue and there was even a gas fireplace, but the coolest thing of all was that this was the actual apartment where Jimi Hendrix had hung out toward the end of his life. Bruce had a connection with Jim Marron, the guy who managed Bearsville studios and who eventually went on to manage Electric Lady, so Bruce had just snagged the apartment of the century. This is where we would stay when we were in the city.

Back in Woodstock, Troy and I were both determined to prepare for this project properly. Even though we knew ahead of time that we would be working on this recording with studio musicians, we still needed to put some kind of band together so that we could rehearse. We were introduced to a young British guy named Derek Foley who played lead guitar. We also had Jim Gregory in our back pocket should we need a bass player for rehearsals. That was what we needed the most: rehearsal, which required more space. We found a two bedroom house on Chestnut Hill Road, in a wooded area just outside of Woodstock village. It had once belonged to a local artist who had left it in his will to our new landlord Bill Barrett. The house on Chestnut Hill had a very large room that was added on. This had been the painter's studio but would make a fine rehearsal space. It had cathedral ceilings and enough floor space to fit a fully equipped band very comfortably. Rick Marotta sent his younger brother Jerry, also a great drummer, to work with us and kind of oversee that we were putting this thing together properly. This project was being done on "spec," or in other words, Rick was producing the demos for no fee with the promise that he would produce the record once our managers got us a deal. He sent his brother Jerry up not only to play with us but also make sure that we had our shit together. Jerry was Rick's watchful eye, so to speak.

The house was situated on Chestnut Hill Road exactly at the place where Witch Tree Road ended. Local mythology had it that the large tree in the clearing at the opposite end of Witch Tree Road was in fact where the locals had hung suspected witches in the 1600's.

There was a nearby stream, a backyard with flowers, trees, and a birdhouse on a high pole. We put together a PA system with microphones, rounded up some amps, and Gerry had brought up a set of drums.

Our session with Rick was scheduled for September so we would have most of the summer to work on the band. We actually booked a few gigs both upstate and on Staten Island. The club on Staten Island was called the Alpine Inn which came complete with a local biker gang called "The Breed." These gentlemen would often stop in for drinks and general mayhem. If we happened to be onstage when these guys arrived, the owner would throw the switch and shut us down. He didn't want any trouble and thought that having a live band playing might be overly stimulating. Actually, he was right. With just the jukebox playing these cretins were much more sedate, having only a few rounds and then getting on their bikes and riding off. At summer's end we were ready.

There was palpable pressure coming from both our managers and Agnes to have this project work well. We were a bit dismayed that our usual rhythm section would not appear on the recording. It would be just me and Troy and Derek Foley, our lead guitarist, but that's the way things were done at the time. Nothing was organic. It was force-fed perfection. Perfect timing, perfect performance, so again that's why Hugh McCracken and Tony Levin were being brought in. They were perfect players.

Into the studio we went, with a most certain intent. After spending countless hours getting drum sounds, we managed to pull the whole four song demo off in just three recording sessions. Mixing the project took another few evenings of work. We would soon have a tape copy in our grubby hands and upon returning to Woodstock we could listen ad nauseam. Now the only thing that we could do was wait. Bruce and David had some work ahead of them.

I was always a bit of a neat freak so I would roam around the house straightening up, rearranging the living room, cleaning dirty ashtrays, that sort of thing. One day after being out for several hours, Troy came home wearing a Cheshire grin on his face beaming with excitement. When I asked him what was up, he answered coyly, "Oh nothing . . . just THIS!" And pulled a .357 Magnum from his jacket pocket. This thing was quite a bit more than any ordinary pistol. The barrel looked to be almost a foot long. "Troy," I said, "that's Dirty fucking Harry!"

I was immediately shaken. I hadn't seen a gun since the 22-gauge rifle I practiced with to get my Marksmanship merit badge back in the Boy Scouts. This is yet another rather stark example of just how different Troy and I were as people. I always considered myself to be somewhat reserved, something of an intellectual, whereas Troy could easily be a troglodyte, a downright heathen. He seemed to delight in being shockingly provocative, putting people on edge, making them feel ill at ease, and firing off a "*flare*" for the dramatic. Just as he had done that night in ODO studios about a year before. He wanted to run with the wolves, having a streak of the devil in him. Hoping to put me at ease he said, "Why don't we go upstairs and shoot it out the window?"

"Well that sounds like a splendid idea, Ollie," I mimicked. All the while in the back of my head I am questioning, "What the fuck?"

We went up to my room, which faced the back of the property, opened the window, and looked around for a target. "The birdhouse!" he said. The small birdhouse was perched on a ten-foot pole and was easily within fifteen yards of the back of the house. He took the first shot and then another and another. Then he turned to me. "You wanna give it a try?" he asked with that same spooky grin. And so, as he likes to tell it, he held back some of the fabric on my kimono so I could have a little more reach. I took careful aim and began to fire. It's a good thing that we weren't drinking because we would have looked for even more targets. When that birdhouse was gone, it was gone . . . just a pole in the ground. "Whoa! That was fun!" we both nearly simultaneously exclaimed. After the shooting match we both turned in for the night.

The following afternoon I decided to do some gardening. I had bought some seeds and was planning to plant them in a small area out back that was surrounded by rocks. Just as I was in the middle of digging up the area inside of the rock circle I heard footsteps coming toward me from behind. "What happened to the birdhouse?" I looked up to see that it was Bill Barrett our landlord standing there.

My voice began to quiver, "Why, I don't . . . really . . . there was a birdhouse?"

"You're damned right there was a birdhouse and what are you doing digging up the garden?" he demanded. I explained that I had planned to restore it by putting in some new flowers. "Haven't you ever heard of perennials? This is a tulip garden," he sternly said, looming over me like he was about to pounce. "You boys are going to pay for that birdhouse!" he shouted, turning away to get back into his car. When I told Troy what had happened we both had a really good laugh. Pistols and tulips. Just too funny!

CHAPTER 11

THE BIG DEAL

It was mid-November, nearly Thanksgiving, the demos came out great and were "in the can" as they say, or in layman's terms, done. Troy and I were sitting around the living room bantering, making fun of each other, laughing and smoking weed. We were getting dreadfully low and I had become proficient at pulling a joint or two out of a pile of seeds that I would sift inside of a shoe box top. We sat gratefully smoking our last joint. Just as that joint burnt down to a roach the phone rang. It was Agnes with some news.

"Bruce and David have secured a record deal and we need you both to drive to the city to meet with the three of us," quickly adding, "And NO lawyers!" Why would she make such a demand unless we were both about to get screwed? I was shocked by her "command," but still had presence enough to ask her which company was interested in signing us. She refused to say but simply asserted that we not try to involve any legal representation. I told her that Troy and I needed to talk and that we would call her back.

Since I took the call, it was on me to explain. "Hey, I think that we can both agree that we need to be signed to a major... right?" I went on, "Listen man, Aggie wouldn't tell me which label she was talking about. This sounds kinda fishy to me!" He agreed. Certainly she may have been wary of us trying to circumvent her and our managers and go to the label directly, but what could have been gained by doing that? We all still needed each other on some level. After some deliberation we both decided that unless she would tell us which label it was then maybe we would decline the offer. Especially concerned with her demand, I couldn't help but wonder if someone else might be whispering in her ear. Could it be that either Bruce, David, or Agnes didn't trust me? Or just maybe somebody didn't trust Troy?

So after we agreed on how to proceed I called Aggie back and said that unless she was willing to tell us who the record label was, our appearance would not be forthcoming. She was really pissed, and before hanging up the phone quickly added, "You're both cut off." That was the end. All the work, the whole summer rehearsing and preparing all gone in a flash with just the click of a phone. Our weekly checks stopped appearing in our mailbox and pretty soon we were broke and were about to run out of heating oil. That December, on my birthday, we were burning our trash in the fireplace in order to keep warm. This was dismal, if not downright tragic. We had come all this way only to be taken by the people we most trusted. Yet another brick wall, this time apparently of my own making. In hindsight, the decision not to walk into a trap was one of cautious self-preservation. It was an attempt to avoid becoming just another rock and roll casualty. We later found out that the proposed deal was with RCA, which would have been a great label for us at the time. Again in hindsight, this was a pivotal moment of self-sabotage in not trusting myself to properly navigate the waters. This time instead of having my mother set me up to fail, I had accomplished it all by myself.

Sandy and Laurie got wind of our situation and began to bring us groceries. We borrowed money from friends to buy another oil delivery, but we were clearly doomed. Sandy and Laurie, quitting their jobs with Albert Grossman, decided that they would move to the city and live in an apartment that Sandy's family had in Greenwich Village right on Bleecker Street. Her grandparents had two apartments in the same building and both were protected by "rent control," which meant that the rent was the same that it was nearly two decades before, in the early fifties, no more than $60 a month.

Troy and I scraped together just enough to rent a truck and we began packing it up with our belongings. We drove off with our stuff without paying our back rent. Feeling hungry we decided that before leaving the area, we would stop at a pancake house in Kingston right by the entrance to the New York Thruway. We sat there eating our breakfast in virtual silence when a voice boomed from behind us. It was Bill Barrett. He had gone by the house in the morning and seen that we had vacated without paying the rent, and had somehow managed to find us cowering at the pancake house. I suppose the open-back truck full of furniture was a fairly good clue. There were some harsh words but we profusely apologized saying that somehow, someday we would make it up to him, but we had just gotten screwed by our alleged "team" and needed to move on. He turned around, satisfied that he had said his piece, and drove away. Troy sometimes carried with him an old lost tooth that he had saved. He used it when we had no money to pay for a meal. This time he dropped it on his plate

complaining to the waiter that he had broken it off while bit-
ing into a piece of toast and sausage at the same time. That last
breakfast was free.

Back in New York, Troy was taken in by his friend Neil
Portman and I headed down to 8th Street with just enough
nerve to knock on Bruce's door. I was surprised to find that in
the midst of Justice's breakup, Derek Foley, our guitarist, had
heard through the grapevine that Bruce was giving up his fabulous village apartment and moving to the upper west side. So
now Derek was living there with his girlfriend, Cathy. They
agreed to let me crash for a while. I stayed in a small second
bedroom. Unfortunately, this arrangement didn't last long. I
had no job and no money so one day Derek simply asked me
to leave. Next I showed up at Sandy and Laurie's door. They
agreed to let me stay but made it clear that they wouldn't support me. I wasn't about to try to get back my old job at Colony.
It would be far too embarrassing to wind up on that doorstep.
Just a step backward when what I needed was more of a side
step. I was feeling discouraged and unsure of myself. So I decided to get a hack license and maybe drive a cab for a while.

I was perhaps the laziest cabdriver the city had ever seen.
I would find myself most days at Thom Kidrin's apartment
watching old movies on TV and smoking weed all afternoon.

Despite this obvious impediment I was still able to con-
tribute some money for groceries and rent but what was really
confusing to me was who I was sleeping with. Sandy and I had
made love a few times back in Woodstock and I had slept with
Laurie as well. Now I was living with both of them.

Nixon had resigned; it was now the mid-seventies. These
were the days of sexual freedom, so at times I would be with
Sandy and when Sandy was with someone else I might be with
Laurie. When Laurie's old boyfriend turned up and stayed for

a few days, I would be back with Sandy again. Not altogether a bad arrangement.

Sandy was slowly becoming disenchanted with being in Manhattan and began talking about how much she missed living in Woodstock. She could easily return, her mom and brother still lived there, so with that, she decided to leave. Laurie's family lived in Brooklyn so she wanted to stay in the city. I just wanted a roof over my head. Sandy assured us that we could probably get away with hanging on to the apartment for a few months before something would have to change. The "rent control" laws in New York City demanded that only a blood relative of the original leaseholder could legally live there, so we had a bit of time before Sandy's grandmother who lived upstairs had to fill the apartment with a niece or nephew.

Uptown, Bruce Henderson was very happily living in a huge three bedroom apartment on West End Avenue at 70th Street. I went to visit him and tried to patch up whatever hard feelings might still be there. He was surprisingly receptive. I think that in retrospect, Bruce always liked me, despite what had gone down. For whatever reason it didn't seem like he blamed me for any part of it. After all was said and done, he was probably able to get a nice tax deduction on the amount of venture capital that he had lost. In fact, he said that I was welcome anytime especially for a game of backgammon, at which I had become quite formidable.

Troy was living only two blocks away from Bruce at the time. His friend Neil Portman had a nice apartment on 72nd Street. Neil had been in the music business on some level, although his track record was never really clear to me. He was tall and thin with curly brown hair and wire-rim glasses. What was clear was that Neil had a bit of money and was now Troy's new manager. He convinced Troy to start using his legal name, Benny Mardones. Benny and I were having an "on again, off again" relationship at the time. There was some undeniable residual tension between us over the Justice debacle. When we were "on again" we would get together to write, but mostly I was writing alone. Naturally I didn't mind; I had started off that way. What concerned me was that my career was stalled, so I began to contemplate my next move.

Laurie had begun looking for an apartment and hinting that she wanted to live alone. Eventually she found a pretty cool garden studio on Hudson Street in the West Village. Oddly enough it too had a rock garden with a man-made stream and bamboo trees, just like Bruce's old place on 8th Street. I really did love Laurie and was secretly hoping that we could stay together. I had already decided that the only thing left for me to do was to go crawling back to E. H. Morris, ask Agnes for her forgiveness, and hope to get my old job back. Hearing that, Laurie became much more receptive to us staying together, so we moved into that tiny studio on Hudson Street.

The Morris office had moved yet again into a smaller suite in a building on 7th Avenue. Surprisingly, Aggie also seemed receptive to having me back in her life. The loss of the RCA deal as well as her legal demands were never spoken of. Oddly though, she asked me if I had seen Ginger. When I told her I hadn't she added, "Well she's been saying some awfully terrible things about me." I had known for some time that Agnes was unhappily married, but being a Catholic, would never entertain the possibility of divorce. I also knew that after Ray vanished, Agnes and Ginger would spend a great deal of time together. Sometimes behind closed doors. Now that Ginger was no longer on the scene, and I had heard rumors that she had "come out," it finally occurred to me that Ginger and Agnes had possibly been lovers. I suppose in her mind my presence would act as an invisible shield against any memory of her "self perceived deviant affair." After all, Aggie was still a good Irish Catholic girl from Queens.

Even with all the gradual downsizing, the Morris office was still a great place to be. People like Harold Arlen would appear to pick up his quarterly check rather than have it mailed.

Mr. Arlen, of course, was responsible for writing many popular standards, but maybe the most famous was "Somewhere Over The Rainbow." I was completely in awe of him. He would appear wearing a tailor-made suit, custom tie, and a carnation in his lapel. He autographed one of his songbooks for me. Of course, there was also the other end of the spectrum, like the old Tin Pan Alley writer Adolph "Buddy" Green, one of three writers of the song "Sentimental Journey" and "Never Never Land." He was more like the Martin Short character who smokes one of those big green cigars and calls for the bandleader to give him a "Bouncy C," quite a persona.

To my surprise, Aggie was willing to help me put another band together built upon my own music. She found an aspiring manager named Tom Kijac, who called himself "Major Tom" after the Bowie song "Space Oddity." I think that Tom accidentally stumbled into E. H. Morris. He was probably looking for some kind of gig at Warner-Chappel Music, which was right next door on the same floor. He helped me put together the band which I named "Monopoly." The lineup went as follows: Jim Gregory on bass, Thommy Price on drums, Tom Morrongiello on rhythm and lead, and Jon Gordon on lead guitar. We began rehearsing at M&R, a rehearsal space on 30th Street.

Major Tom had it in his head that we would get the New Year's Eve gig at a very hot club called Trax. "I'm gonna get you this gig for real," he would say in an exaggerated voice, his eyes getting big. The club was located on West 72nd Street and was one flight below street level. A "who's who" crowd would normally turn up to hang in their VIP room. We needed to play a few gigs before that could happen. Tom eventually booked us into a club called Home on the upper east side. He invited the guy who booked Trax to come see the band. After the set, Tom ran over to us all excited, waving his arms and yelling, "You got the gig! You got it! You got it."

This was unbelievable! Nobody just gets a New Year's Eve gig at the hottest club in the city, but we did. I'm still not sure how and why all this was clicking. I would like to think that I was becoming more secure as a front man. I was no longer playing second fiddle to Troy or Benny or whoever he was now.

1977 New Year's Eve at Trax was a very hot ticket and not anyone could simply stroll in. The room was filling up with celebrities; half of the cast of *Saturday Night Live* was there. Rock stars and TV and film personalities were littering the venue.

To say that I was nervous would be an understatement, but I was equally determined to make a splash. This time I was truly ready. Monopoly was my band. When the curtains opened we popped like a fucking firecracker, whipping into a thirty-minute set that was built to blow the doors off. Even though we were completely unknown, from the very first note we had the audience's attention and we never let go. I was all over the stage. We started getting rowdy applause after each tune. At one point near the end of our set, with the mic in my hand, I actually stepped off the stage onto someone's table. I think I might have knocked over somebody's drink. We were brought back for two encores. We had really killed it. Backstage after the set the dressing room door burst open and in walked John Belushi. Major Tom reached for his little pocket mirror and his coke stash and proceeded to lay out about a half a gram, offering Belushi a line. John just grabbed the mirror and snorted the whole thing in one fell swoop. I thought Tom's eyes were going to spring right out of his head. Belushi hung out with us in the dressing room for quite a while just joking around and generally entertaining us. I was basking in glory. I had come and with the band's help, I had conquered. This all served to take me right back to my early childhood days at Little Theatre and Grandma's Cafe. I was fueled by the audience. I was once again filled with the love that I had always felt was missing at home.

That was truly Monopoly's greatest shining moment, but because of personnel problems, between the two competing lead guitarists, it would also be its last, but just the same, things were beginning to change. I could feel the universe shifting in my direction.

CHAPTER 12

NEVER NEVER LAND

Lee Eastman was legal counsel for E. H. Morris; he was also the father of John and Linda Eastman. His son John practiced law alongside his father while Linda; a photographer, would become the wife of Paul McCartney. McCartney had learned the value of owning publishing rights the hard way, so he set about hunting down and buying up music catalogs. He had his eye on E. H. Morris and its rich theatrical history.

One afternoon in late spring, I was sitting in one of the smaller offices working on a song when the door flew open and in slid a very inebriated Buddy Morris. His suit was wrinkled, he held a glass of scotch in one hand, and both his tie and his zipper were halfway down. "You're Davy, right?" he slurred.

"Yes sir, I am, and it's very nice to finally meet you," I said, somewhat shocked.

"So what do YOU think? Should I sell this company or not?" he slurred again. I was about to say "no," but instead insisted that I really couldn't comment. After all it was his company.

"Well," he went on, "they're offering me somewhere around nine million bucks and my two sons are hot for their money... so I think I'm gonna sell." Nine million dollars sounded like a lot of money, but also not. The company owned so many famous theatrical productions from *Hello, Dolly!* to *A Chorus Line*, *Annie* to *Grease*, not to mention a host of classic standards, so in perspective a nine million dollar payday seemed mind-bogglingly low.

However, that is exactly what transpired. The company was sold to MPL Communications (McCartney Paul and Linda) for a pittance of its true value. The contents of this great company could now be easily confined to a single filing cabinet. Everyone lost their jobs and the doors were locked. That was it. It was over. The entire face of the music industry was changing before my eyes. It was becoming even more cutthroat than ever before.

I went to the studio apartment on Hudson Street and delivered the somber news to Laurie. I knew that it was only a matter of time until she would ask me to move out having no income, so I began looking for work. I found a job waiting on tables in a place called Hopper's over on 6th Avenue. I was a terrible waiter. In retrospect, I think that I was blaming innocent patrons for the fact that I was actually having to work a miserable menial day job. I would let people sit waiting forever before I would even appear at their table. Once I placed their order and I might have just lit a cigarette in the kitchen when the chef put the hot order up, I would calmly finish my cigarette before bringing the meal to the table. I simply didn't give a shit. For some reason the manager liked me just the same and I actually lasted there for several months before being shown the door.

I got a surprise call from Benny one day in mid-1978, saying that he really needed my help. His manager Neil wanted to take us out to L.A. to put a band together around Benny. We were to rehearse at S.I.R., where the big boys rehearsed. Whoever might be in town to play an arena-sized venue would usually rehearse at S.I.R. We would be staying at the famous Chateau Marmont on Sunset Boulevard. This sounded exciting to me so I went along for the ride. The Marmont was a strange place, very much a "Hollywood Babylon" kind of vibe. It was the hotel that would become even more famous in the early eighties as the place where John Belushi, who I'd spent that New Year's Eve with, would die of a heroin overdose.

Neil had rented all of us a large suite that included a kitchen. Benny and I decided that we needed some groceries so we ventured over to Ralph's Supermarket on Sunset. We had a two-page shopping list which we split. I went off to search for the items on my list. Starting down one of the aisles, I saw someone who looked strangely familiar. "That's Jeremy," I said to myself in total disbelief. "Oh my God, find Benny." Those memories of the writers' hangs back at the Morris town house came rushing back. Especially the night that Richard Porterfield told us that Jeremy was dead. I ran over a few aisles and spotted Benny putting items into a cart. "Benny . . . Benny you gotta come with me," I insisted.

"What's going on now?" he sing-song muttered, as if he was being disturbed.

"Just fucking come with me," I said, pulling him over to the aisle where I thought that I had seen Jeremy. "Benny . . . look at that guy! That's Jeremy!" Benny just stood there murmuring, "Jeremy's supposed to be dead." We both slowly walked toward him. Jeremy was stuffing his pockets with anything that would fit. He was stumbling around the aisle with an apple in one hand and a can of Coke in the other, which I suppose he intended to pay for. "Hey Jeremy . . . it's us . . . remember?" I said. He looked up, glassy-eyed, and said, "Oh . . . Hey . . . Troy . . . what are you guys doing here?" He was ripped . . . totally "downed" out. We wanted to help, so we put all kinds of food into a cart for him and checked out, taking him with us. We asked him to let us drive him home with the groceries. Eventually we wound up in a part of town that I would never return to. He had a studio apartment far off in the bowels of East L.A. with a mattress on the floor. The place was dark and filthy and smelled of urine. In the end we had no choice but to leave him there, both of us teary-eyed, we returned to the hotel.

Our stay in L.A. would soon come to an abrupt end, as the whole project just seemed to fall apart. Something had apparently gone wrong on Neil's end. It seemed like whatever he had set up in advance for Benny had suddenly caved in. Yet another brick wall. Benny's manager needed to come up with a plan B and fast.

Back in New York, about a month later Benny called to tell me that Neil had finally come through. He had potentially gotten him a record deal and he would be cutting some of our songs. The only downside was that he hadn't signed with a major label. The deal was with Private Stock records, a small independent label started by Larry Uttal after he had been ousted from Bell records. This little indie label had become somewhat successful with the likes of Rupert Holmes and Cissy Houston, yet it seemed like a home for one-hit wonders. Just the same I was very happy for Benny and offered my help in any way that I could. I wound up doing background vocals on the record, which was produced by Andrew Loog Oldham, the famous onetime manager and producer of the Rolling

Stones. "Loog," as he was often called, had married Esther Farfan, a Colombian actress. At the time it was rumored that Mr. Oldham had a steady supply of golf balls shipped directly to his apartment from Bogota fully stuffed with cocaine. Oddly enough the record was to be cut at Bearsville studios just outside of Woodstock, our old stomping grounds. Mick Ronson of David Bowie fame would be adding lead guitar. It was strange to be back in Woodstock. Especially given these new circumstances. This was Benny's project and although our songs were being recorded, we were no longer a team. I was simply doing backup vocals on a project that was so laden with cocaine that the phrase "forty yard line" took on new meaning.

At the beginning of each session a line of blow was laid out from one end of the recording console to the other, just below each of the track faders. Consequently, the first mixes sounded more like Mono than Stereo. I had actually helped Benny get this deal. When he auditioned for Larry Uttal, he had everyone come to his apartment. A small crowd had squeezed into Benny's living room to listen. I accompanied him on piano and guitar and added vocals, just like we had done back in Aggie's office a year or so earlier. When the set was done, Benny didn't even introduce me as cowriter. It was all about him. What really hit me the most was being tossed to the sidelines. I still felt responsible for blowing the RCA deal. So once again I was feeling the sting of self-sabotage. Something I had learned all too well and had become quite proficient at.

Benny's first solo LP entitled *Thank God for Girls*, after copious remixing, was finally released in 1978 to mixed reviews and tepid sales numbers, but it was enough to get Benny's name out there. Naturally I was very happy that some of our songs had finally been recorded and released.

As good as this news was it would also signal the beginning of Benny's fall from grace. Two years from the release of his first solo project, he signed with Polygram records and in 1980 would release his second LP *Never Run Never Hide.* He would also wind up recording even more of our songs for that record. Benny began to "freebase" cocaine. I was certainly no stranger to coke but freebase was a whole different thing than simply snorting it up the nose. This new development frightened me a bit so I began to distance myself from him. Benny eventually turned to a new cowriter, Robert Tepper. Some of our mutual friends called Tepper, "Bobby Come Lately," as everybody knew that Benny and I were the "original" writing team. Despite that, they wrote a song that was to become Benny's biggest hit, "Into The Night," a very breezy, mid-tempo, blue-eyed soul record that became an instant radio classic.

The late seventies and early eighties was the height of the cocaine explosion in New York. Freebase is highly addictive and for Benny it became an immediate problem. It's also the least economical method of consuming cocaine, but it packs a wallop. The coke is washed with ammonia, freeing it of hydrochloride which returns it to its alkaloid chemical "base," cocaine sulfate. What's left is a rock of coke that can be vaporized in a glass pipe accomplished by igniting a butane flame apparatus sometimes called a "cubby." The high is instantaneous and extremely intense, but lasts for only a very short time. Then you "crash" and find yourself preparing another hit. One could perform this process "endlessly" as long as the blow held out. Benny had moved up to my old neighborhood, Washington Heights. I recall visiting him once and walking into a littered apartment, cigarette butts and discarded clothing strewn all about on the floor. There was an unfamiliar and somewhat foreboding smell in the air. A faint waft of ammonia. Benny was looking pale and grey in the only real light that the apartment offered, which seemed to come from the television in his bedroom. I didn't stay.

A week or two later, he called me at home at four thirty in the morning, saying that he would be waiting downstairs at my apartment and that I should join him. When I reached the lobby there was a long black limousine parked in front of my building. He and his girlfriend beckoned to me from inside. Once seated, he put a glass pipe in my mouth and fired it up. I took a very long hit not even realizing the potency of the amount I was inhaling. Suddenly I became extremely nauseous and opening the car door, I vomited onto the street. Closing the door of the limo I remember seeing the chauffeur's shoulders dart up to his ears as if to say, "Oh shit, I hope this asshole didn't just throw up all over the backseat." I began seeing less and less of Benny as he spiraled into serious abuse. At one point he had a habit of about a thousand dollars a day. I imagined that he would soon have a couple of Colombian nationals knocking on his door demanding that he stay current with cash.

I hated to see this happen to him. I seem to remember being a part of some kind of unsuccessful intervention on his behalf. It didn't occur to me at the time that I too would be falling off my own cliff. It wouldn't be very long before my own life would be defined by drinking and doing blow.

On a warm afternoon, I was walking in the Village not far from the apartment when I heard someone yell, "Hey Gary!" Nobody called me Gary anymore, still I turned around to see this guy just standing there with a giant smile on his face waving at me. As I walked toward him I began to remember his face from Peddie. He was the roommate of a friend of mine and I remember talking to him a few times when I would stop by to visit my friend. Sometimes his roommate wouldn't show and we wound up having long and engaging conversations. After all, he was yet another kid from Jersey. "It's Jonathan . . . Jonathan Holtsman, remember?" he said with that smile. "Yeah of course I remember you, man . . . how're you doing?" I said, shaking his hand. He explained that he was an aspiring songwriter, had remembered that I was as well and told me that he was running a songwriter showcase out of the back room of a midtown restaurant. He also mentioned that he was living over on 16th Street not far from where I lived and that I should come by and hang out. We exchanged phone numbers and I promised to call him. Benny's first release had faded into obscurity. I was going from one part-time job to another just to keep some cash flow. Laurie and I were still living in that tiny studio on Hudson Street. During the evenings I was busily writing songs and listening to the likes of Elvis Costello, Graham Parker, Nick Lowe, and the Sex Pistols for inspiration in my own work. I called up Jonathan and he invited me to check out his writer's showcase, so I made the journey uptown.

It took place every Tuesday night and when I got there the room was full of not only songwriters but ordinary people who were actually there to listen. I was surprised that something like this was happening in midtown Manhattan when one would expect it to be so much more of a downtown kind of thing. I sat for a while to check out the talent and was pleasantly surprised that these writers were all fairly good at their craft; in fact, there wasn't a crumb bun among them. So I too became a regular.

One night after doing a short three song set, a thin, well-dressed older woman introduced herself to me as Judy Berger, an entertainment attorney. She told me how much she enjoyed my songs. We made a bit of small talk, I thanked her for her encouraging words, and that was pretty much it. For a moment it kind of felt like something was about to happen, but apparently not. I later asked Jonathan about Judy. He told me that she often attended his showcase and, as far as he knew, was actively scouting for new undiscovered talent.

I visited Jonathan several times at his apartment and after a while he introduced me to a few of his neighbors. I met Randy Rolin who was a horn player/cab driver/coke dealer, and another neighbor, a lovely girl named Barbara Denhoff who was a dancer. Eventually Jonathan met a cute but slightly neurotic girl named Tina, who was brought by her friends to the showcase for her birthday, and she was quite inebriated. Her friends managed to get her home but Jonathan began to date her after that initial bleary-eyed introduction. Eventually he moved out of his place on 16th Street and he and Tina moved into a nice apartment on Bank Street around the corner from where I was living. Barbara Denhoff would often show up at the showcase on Tuesday nights, and eventually we slept together. I stayed in touch with Randy just in case I ever needed a gram or an eight ball, never realizing that I would eventually become rather intimate with the interior of his apartment.

This new pop/rock movement was certainly speaking my language. I continued to listen extensively and write like a madman. Laurie was now working for Sam Hood. Talk about full circle, Sam had once managed the Gaslight where I first performed in New York City. Hood had become an artist manager. Laurie worked as Sam's secretary/assistant. He was handling a new "super group" called Fotomaker. This band was composed of Gene Cornish and Dino Danelli, both from the Young Rascals, along with Wally Bryson who was in the Raspberries and a young Frankie Vinci. Their road manager, Jon Small, had once worked with Billy Joel. Jon, years before, had secured some friends in the business while their band Atilla was briefly signed to Epic records. Jon was the drummer for the duo that he and Billy had formed after they left The Hassles.

I had carefully put some of my new songs on cassette, just me singing and playing guitar but trying to capture the feel of punk and new wave which I had fallen so in love with. Particular new acts like Elvis Costello, Graham Parker, and Nick Lowe were not only very melodic but also quite intellectual. Of course at the very same time I was really attracted to the "balls to the wall" sound of the Sex Pistols and the Ramones. I played the tape for Laurie and surprisingly she said that she would bring it with her to the office and test it out on Sam and maybe some of the guys in the band. Jon Small heard the cassette and showed some interest, at least enough to have Laurie bring me by the office so we could meet.

I sat down with Jon at Sam Hood's office and he told me that he thought my presentation was pretty good, especially given that it was so stark and had no production value. He asked me to let him run with the tape to see if he might be able to get some interest. I agreed, but I couldn't help but reflect on all the brick walls that I had encountered up to this point. Somehow I could still find the bright side. Somewhere I still had faith that I would achieve my goal.

Jon apparently had thought to go straight back to Columbia records to his old friend, Don DeVito, who had done some work with Dylan. Within a week or so I got a call from Jon, "Hey man, could you put some players together for a CBS demo thing?" Naturally, I had no trouble with that at all. I already had a sizable pool of musicians to choose from. So Jon and I along with Thommy Price on drums, Joe Vasta on bass, and Tom Morrongiello on lead guitar, began to organize. This would be a simple three song demo. We were to do this project in the old CBS recording studio on the East side of Manhattan.

When I walked into what was simply a very large room I could feel the history. Benny Goodman, Tony Bennett, and Frank Sinatra had all recorded here as well as countless others. It was an open space with very high ceilings and no sound separation except for the movable walls on wheels called "gobos." You would arrange the gobos in a certain way to encapsulate whatever it was that you wanted to separate from whatever else was being recorded. The engineer looked like he had been working there forever. He was a throwback to the days of yesteryear, a caricature, wearing yellow plaid pants, a white patent leather belt which could barely be seen under his protruding belly. He sat at the console smoking a cigar like he had already seen and heard it all. He probably had.

We were well rehearsed and expected the session to go quickly. The proposed "single" was a song called "Listen to the Heartbeat," which was very upbeat with serious attitude, practically punk. Nick Lowe had this very cool song called "Heart of the City." I listened to it over and over and I think it was the main inspiration for "Heartbeat." We didn't end up with the kind of sound quality that we might have hoped for but the energy was phenomenal. At Don DeVito's suggestion, Jon submitted the demo to Greg Geller, who was an A&R rep at Columbia probably best known for having signed Elvis Costello. This seemed like a good move, although I didn't want to be perceived as a Costello knockoff. We waited a few weeks and heard nothing so Jon decided to take the tape elsewhere, even though CBS had paid for it and allegedly had the right of "first refusal." We went to Mercury where we encountered some interest from Steve Katz, who was an original member of The Blues Project, Al Kooper's band. Steve had a giant Lemmon 714 Quaalude paperweight on his desk, an open reminder of the 'Coke and Quaalude' culture of the day. Then we ventured on to Bob Feiden at Arista. Bob was a flamboyant gay gentleman who knew just what his boss liked. Upon first hearing the tape he went completely nuts. He in turn played the demo for the legendary Clive Davis who gave it the green light. The next thing I knew we were in negotiations. Through Jonathan Holtsman, I got in touch with Judy Berger, the attorney who had spoken to me that night at the songwriter's showcase and had also become legal representation for Fotomaker, Sam Hood's new band. She agreed to represent me and immediately jumped in. Just as all this wheeling and dealing began to really heat up, Greg Geller called Jon to say that Columbia was interested in signing me. Stop right there, I immediately began to think that we should back out of the Arista deal and go with Columbia. I had been warned by friends in the business that Clive could easily turn on you. He was completely ego driven. Plus CBS had more of a reputation with artist development. They normally wouldn't drop an artist if the first release wasn't a gigantic hit. Plus they had "first refusal," or so I thought. Jon insisted that we already had a "bird in the hand" and after all it was Clive "fucking" Davis who wanted to sign me, and how could I possibly resist the charms of Clive? Against my better instincts, I relented and the Arista deal proceeded.

CHAPTER 13

ARISTA

In the fall of '79, we put together a showcase for Arista which was held at Starsound on Lafayette Street in lower Manhattan. Judy, wanting to impress, had the affair catered. Starsound was a brand-new rehearsal facility that everyone wanted to work in. They had several nice rooms and a killer showcase room which was large enough to seat thirty people. The stage was tall and wide and fully equipped with a top of the line PA system, great amps, and a fine set of Rodgers drums. The private audition for Clive Davis would be set here. I harkened back to Baggie's and playing for John Hammond, even though Clive Davis and Hammond were two very different people. Our lead guitarist, Tom Morrongiello, had to drop out at the very last minute, but he had the grace and good sense to give a cassette copy of our set to a young guitarist who just happened to be there working with another act in one of the other rehearsal rooms. As it turned out, Robert Sarzo was a fine lead guitarist. He happened to be the younger brother of Rudy Sarzo, the bassist for Quiet Riot. He used his Walkman to learn the tunes and presented himself as being quite ready for the showcase. A limousine pulled up to the door on Lafayette Street. The back door was opened by the driver and out stepped a small balding man with sunglasses. He was in a fine tailored suit and was accompanied by a rather thin gentleman who had a "more than seasonal" tan. This was Clive Davis and Bob Fieden. After some pleasantries were exchanged with Judy and Jon, they all proceeded to the showcase room. Even with the last-minute addition of Robert Sarzo on lead guitar the set was flawless. I hurled all of my energy directly at Clive who occupied the center seat in the third row. The whole thing was a huge success and Clive was completely convinced. In the end that was all that mattered.

A few weeks later, record producer Jimmy Iovine was having a "sit down" with Clive regarding another artist that Mr. Davis wanted him to produce. During the course of that meeting, Clive played my demo for Jimmy who immediately said, "No, I wanna do this!"

Naturally, on its face, this was all very positive and quite exciting, but in reality the vultures were circling the camp. I sensed that there was something unseen afoot. Something odd and possibly even traitorous. I wasn't sure what it was but I could feel it and it made me feel very wary.

Judy Berger's office was high atop a midtown skyscraper. It was finely wood paneled with a matching desk and very comfortable black leather chairs for her clients. It was also a bit messy with stacks of papers all over her desk while other piles were haphazardly placed on the windowsill. During a meeting with Judy and Jon, as they were talking, I walked over to the window of her office to take in the view of the midtown skyline against the grey rainy day. I looked to the stereo speaker on my right and saw a one page document lying on top. Just eyeballing it very quickly I was able to see that Judy and Jon were aligning to split a percentage. I wasn't really sure what this meant unless they were planning to actually form a limited partnership. As Judy was in fact my attorney this development surprised me. Feeling uncertain, I walked over and took a seat. Jon paused and turned to me and said that he needed to explain something. "Judy is MY attorney now . . . do you understand?" He spoke in a manner that one might speak to a dog or someone who was partially deaf or stupid. "So now, you must go out and get your own attorney," he continued. I just sat there very uncomfortably and absorbed this strange turn of events.

No one was really explaining anything to me, they were simply talking at me. So were Judy and Jon already trying to screw me when nothing had actually even happened yet? I had no one to turn to here. Nobody to confide in. Quite unsettled, I headed downtown not knowing what to do.

I knew some friends who had some dealings with Joseph Serling, an up-and-coming entertainment attorney, so I thought to ask him to jump in and take over. Luckily Joe was available and he was tenacious and hungry. Serling was thin, sported a beard and glasses, and had a tuna melt on rye for lunch every day. His favorite catchphrase for describing bullshit was "Yadda Yadda," and he wasn't afraid to get down and dirty. Somehow between Judy Berger and Joe Serling a two-album "firm" deal was negotiated on my behalf with Arista.

Clive played the demo at an Arista convention in Miami to tumultuous applause, so this was all actually happening and it was big. I was feeling like I was finally at the doorstep of success. Soon Jimmy Iovine began the courting process by introducing us to his engineer Shelly Yakus, who I liked immediately. Shelly had a very long list of credits but had recently done the *Easter* LP for Patti Smith and he and Jimmy had just wrapped up *Damn The Torpedoes* for Tom Petty. They had both become major players. That last project piqued my interest because I knew that Petty was a Rickenbacker freak like me, and I very much wanted that classic "Rick" sound. Shelly had a very large boat, or a small yacht, docked in a marina by the River House on the East side. We all met up there one afternoon for a little trip around the Hudson. Jimmy didn't talk to me all that much, he concentrated mostly on Jon. All the time in the back of my head I was thinking that something wasn't right. Since Shelly was piloting the boat, I was basically by myself. I stood on the bow alone and watched as the boat broke the water. Even in the middle of all this new excitement there lurked feelings of tension and treachery. I tried to ignore them and press on.

Finally sometime in late 1979 this project took hold. Once again I was back in studio B at the Record Plant. Recording the "basics" for the record seemed to take forever, the "basics" meaning just the basic track of bass, drums, and possibly one guitar, and everything else was an "overdub." Jimmy had us do what seemed like thirty takes or more for each of the ten songs and I sang with the band on every single take. Although other producers of the day used a similar approach to tracking, the most infamous probably being Mutt Lange who produced Def Leppard's *Pyromania*, it was grueling almost to the point of cruelty. After the basics were finally finished, Jimmy started showing up less and less to the studio. It actually got to the point where he would simply ring up Shelly at around 10:00 PM and ask, "What's done?" His absence had become more than painfully obvious to me and it seemed very odd. Why would a producer choose not to be present during the process of his own project? Jon Small, my manager, leveraged Jimmy's disappearing act to press him for coproduction credit. And it worked. Everyone seemed to be taking care of themselves.

When it came time for me to do my vocals, my voice was shot. I needed to see a doctor. When the ENT looked at my throat he was taken aback. He examined me only to say, "It looks like you've been screaming at the top of your lungs for a month. The lining of your throat is completely inflamed." He told me to try not to speak at all for a week and give it plenty of rest for a month thereafter. He then painted my vocal cords with Jensen Violet and gave me a prescription for an antibiotic. Despite this we kept going by adding every guitar solo or part that was needed and as my voice got better I was able to do background vocals against the "dummy" vocal that had already been recorded.

When Jimmy would actually show up, he would spend an inordinate amount of time on the phone. He seemed to be distracted like there might be something going on in his personal life at the time that few knew about. He and I never spoke on a personal level, in fact we rarely spoke at all. I felt his detachment and I wasn't sure what was going on. I suppose that I wanted his attention and maybe even his approval, but I was so pissed about the way things were going that I told myself that I didn't care. It didn't matter. The same psychological tactics that I had used on myself as a kid to get through my mother's tyrannical episodes.

My first solo record, *This Day and Age*, was released on Arista records in February of 1980. Despite all the hoopla about this project the record release party was incredibly low-key. It was nothing more than a casual gathering/listening party held in the lounge at the Record Plant just adjacent studio B. All the usual suspects were in attendance, including Clive, Jimmy, the band, and a number of our close friends. It actually seemed to be little more than a nonevent. The single "Listen to the Heartbeat" became a *Billboard* magazine Top 40 hit and made it into the Top Ten on the local charts in New York, Boston, and Philadelphia as well as Cleveland, Detroit, and Chicago. It was funny but also kind of strange when I would listen to the radio at home. The DJs would play "Heartbeat," announce my name, and sometimes talk about me. I remember one night listening to them speculate as to what the "L" in "D. L." stood for. The DJs sounded like they might have been a bit toasted, when one of them suggested that the "L" stood for "latitudinal" and they both started belly laughing.

We began playing around the New York City area. We were booked for two consecutive nights at the Ritz, Jerry Brandt's gigantic rock club, and at the Bottom Line for two back-to-back shows on a night that happened to be right in the middle of a transit strike. No subways in the city of New York were running. We were all concerned that nobody would show. I remember being backstage hearing people's voices and rustling noises, so I peered out from the wings. How did they all get here? That night both shows were sold out. The second show went on well past one in the morning and was simultaneously broadcast in New York, Philly, and Boston on WNEW, WPLJ, and WCOZ respectively. I was told that our three city simulcast was the first of its kind. We did three encores of a new song called "Cold War" which wasn't even on the album, but we had performed it at previous shows. It seemed that night the audience just wouldn't let us go. The record was really breaking in the metropolitan markets. If Arista was indeed looking for the next Graham Parker or Elvis Costello,

I'm pretty sure that they believed they had just found him. I'm also fairly sure that the label was already patting itself on the back because this record was so damn hot right out of the box. They were expecting really big things to simply just happen on their own.

Then, almost immediately, we found ourselves preparing for a real tour. I was dead asleep when the phone rang. It was Jon. "Hey man, we've been picked up as an opening act for two major coliseum tours. We're heading out on the road for at least six weeks or more." Jon rented a Winnebago for the band to travel in and our roadies had their own van with all of our equipment. We would be jumping back and forth from two different tours that were both supporting newly released records at the time. Bob Geldof was enjoying moderate success with his band The Boomtown Rats' *Fine Art of Surfacing* LP, and Bob Seger was topping the charts with *Against the Wind*. Most of these venues were coliseum sized with maybe fifteen to twenty thousand seats. This was a lot to take in and process but man, I was trippin'!

Our first gig was with the Rats at the Tower Theatre in Philadelphia, with around a five-thousand seat capacity. We pulled into a particularly shady side of Philly with our Winnebago, just in time for sound check. This was the biggest venue that I had played thus far. From the stage, the room looked black, but I knew the audience was out there. I could feel them, I could hear them breathing, and then I took a breath. We ripped into the set with raw energy and power and the crowd gave it right back to us, cheering almost as loudly as we were playing. But when we got to the very last number something happened. Suddenly I couldn't hear myself. My monitor was out. I panicked. My mind was racing. What was going on? I couldn't hear myself, all I could hear was my heart pounding. Apparently, the guy running the stage monitors was told to cut the upstage wedges, which meant that the monitors near where I stood were turned off. I kept calling to the crowd, "Can you hear me?!"

"Yes!!" they shouted. I smelled sabotage and stepped back toward the band so I could at least hear what key I was supposed to be singing in. It actually worked. When the song was done and the audience was going wild, I grabbed the microphone and held it by the cable and started over to the side of the stage where the sound engineer was hiding in the wings. I pretended like I was going to throw the mic until he actually walked on stage to try to retrieve it. As soon as he got a quarter way out I swung it over, aiming for his feet . . . I made my mark. The mic was "live," so it made a pretty loud "thump." "You're gonna pay for that, you asshole," he yelled. We left the stage laughing. I had heard stories of big acts perpetrating sabotage upon their opening acts. I wondered if it wasn't Geldof himself who had given this instruction. He hadn't really had a hit since "I Don't Like Mondays," so for him to have the stage crew pull the monitors on us wasn't that surprising. In hindsight though, I have to wonder just how insecure you have to be to do something like that.

Since we were in Philadelphia and close to my hometown, the very best part of that night was all of my childhood friends showing up backstage. Most of them had gone on to enjoy more "normal" pursuits and lifestyles. Ed Dondero, John Grassman, and Arthur Ostroff and a few others had managed to get past security and come to the dressing room to give me congratulatory hugs. That was such a sweet moment. It reminded me of playing back at Grandma's coffeehouse in Glassboro so many years before. To look back and remember that moment made me realize just how far I had come. The following few gigs were with Seger's Silver Bullet Band. We met up with them in Fayetteville, North Carolina, home to Fort Bragg, the US military base. All we got was a "drum check" not an actual "sound check," but the band was so tight by that point that a drum check would do.

I walked out on stage that night to a sea of crew cuts. Nearly the entire audience was military. We were wearing garish clothing and looking dangerously urban. I remember going to Canal Jeans in downtown Manhattan and buying clothes for the band. I had picked out a number of brightly colored shirts for them to wear and urged them to put on skinny black jeans and boots. I would accompany a bright shirt with a vintage black blazer and slip on my "Beatle" boots. We definitely did not fit in with this Fayetteville crowd. I thought for sure someone would try to pop an empty bottle of Jack Daniels off my head. Nothing could have been further from the truth—the audience loved the show. They gave us some serious applause for "Listen to the Heartbeat" which I'm guessing was already in their ears every day.

Back at the hotel later that night, Seger's band was up to no good. The sax player was throwing cherry bombs in the corridor. Some others were having fun banging on the doors of unsuspecting hotel guests. It wasn't quite like the stories you might have heard of hurling TV's out of hotel windows into the swimming pool, but it was pretty raucous and very funny. Bob never participated in any of that nonsense. He was soft-spoken and always treated us with respect. During the tour I would see him in the morning eating breakfast while reading the New York Times at the hotel restaurant. We never really conversed other than to simply acknowledge each other. I didn't want to disturb his meal.

Next it was off to Cleveland, Ohio, and a reunion with the Boomtown Rats. We were staying at the famous Jim Swingo's Hotel which was *the* place to stay. Oddly enough, Englebert Humperdinck was performing in town and staying there as well. He might have been the true antithesis of what we were, but somehow we had been thrown into the same moment in time as though we each occupied the same space in some parallel universe. The lobby was a sea of blue-haired old ladies, adding to the moment's surrealistic nature. Rounding out the mix was our own growing band of groupies. They were easy to spot, dressed with accentuation on fashion and usually quite made-up. It didn't seem to matter if they were there for the Rats or for us. They were interested in conquest. These women would somehow manage to get backstage or find out which local hotel we were staying at. When we checked in, there was a girl sitting on the floor in the hallway right next to my room. There might be a good deal of extracurricular sex ahead and the adolescent in me was shooting for straight A's.

Since we would be opening for the Rats again, I didn't want a repeat of the "sabotage" thing to happen. We needed a plan. So I organized an informal band meeting and told everybody, "We really need to do something about this but I can't be directly involved." I suggested that after the sound check in Cleveland that they all wait back at the hotel by the elevator banks for either the band or the crew to come out and then jump them. They agreed and prepared to pounce. Back in the day, it wasn't unusual to carry a switchblade or stiletto. Every guy in my band was from Staten Island by way of Brooklyn with the exception of Robert, and they all carried knives. The elevator doors opened and the Rat's stage crew stepped out only to have my band appear from behind putting switchblades to their throats saying, "We're from fucking Brooklyn, man, and we will cut you!" These Brits turned whiter than they actually were. This sort of behavior wasn't unusual "on the road." I heard stories about David Lee Roth of Van Halen having the band's security grab the lead singer from the opening act, drag him out to the parking lot, and beat the living shit out of him. Intimidation and sabotage were fairly commonplace. It was dog-eat-dog and only the top dog got the bone.

The next morning I was scheduled for an "on air" interview at WMMS Cleveland with Kid Leo, probably the most popular DJ in local rock radio. As I was entering the building Bob Geldof was coming in as well. He was going to a "taped interview" with a station underling. On the steps up to the building's entrance he glared at me for a moment and then went inside. Bob was not happy. The show that night was seamless and tomorrow would be Chicago, Illinois. When we arrived for sound check the next day in Chicago, the roadies and various tech people were walking by, addressing me as "Mr. Byron" and asking if everything was okay, in particular the monitors. Well we had won the battle but lost the war. We were all taken out for dinner before the show by Mike Bone, who was head of radio promo for Arista. He had been flown out especially to meet with us. Sitting next to me at dinner, he leaned over to me saying, "You know if this record doesn't immediately start to do better your tour support will be pulled." Why didn't this weasel simply say that it was over and if it was, *why* was it over? Was Arista having problems promoting D. L. Byron? Were they just relying on "in-house" promo and hadn't bothered to hire any "outside" promotion? Maybe they thought that it would just sell itself right out of the box. It wasn't as if the label had to polish a turd, they actually had a nugget. My Manager? He didn't say very much.

The last gig was Detroit. I had succumbed to the reality that we would not tour any farther than this. No one had my back and I was sick to my stomach. The gig went well, we got into the Winnebago (by now with comic slur, nicknamed the "Wooden Bagel"), and drove home to New York. Joe Vasta our bass player drove much of the way. Joe liked to drive big things.

Looking back, having the plug pulled may have actually saved my life. I often wonder if things had gotten progressively bigger just how would I have handled it. Having no real support structure in my life at that time, I could have easily ended up just another burnt-out star found by one of his "close friends" lying on the bathroom floor, having succumbed to a heroin overdose. Maybe someone was looking out for me and my life was possibly being spared.

When I first signed on with Arista, Laurie found us a new place on 12th Street off Abington Square in Greenwich Village. It was a very nice one bedroom with a fireplace and a big bath. Tired and road weary, that's where I arrived. She was in bed half awake. She had permed her hair and it looked very sexy. I put down my bags and we made love, which was just what I needed.

Sex on the road was great fun, but this was special, somehow much better. Or I suppose it would be more accurate to say that this kind of love was the most that I felt deserving of in my life at that time. Laurie and I already had a history of cheating on each other. I always knew when she was with someone else and I never made any grand efforts to hide my indiscretions. Life on the road is not easy. I needed every drink, every line, and every fuck that I had, but now it was time to come down.

After this abrupt end of the tour I was spent, disillusioned, and somewhat depressed. I needed some regularity in my daily life but first I was very much in need of a vacation. We planned a trip to Cozumel for a week of sun and relaxation.

One of our encore numbers was a punk remake of the Joe South song "Down in the Boondocks" made famous by Billy Joe Royal. We had kind of "Ramoned" it, by speeding it up and turning it into something that was recognizable as punk rock. Before Laurie and I left for vacation there was some buzz about trying to do a version of that song as a twelve-inch single. The hope was that it might revive LP sales. We shipped off to Mexico and I forgot all about it all for a while.

CHAPTER 14

SPIRITS AND SHADOWS

O ur week together in Mexico was perfect. The beaches of Cozumel were beautiful. We relaxed, rented a scooter, and traveled all over the island in search of the best ceviche. On the day before we were scheduled to leave we got a pretty bad scare. We were swimming not very far from shore, and everything seemed fine when suddenly the sky grew very dark, the winds kicked up, and we both realized that we were in a current that was taking us out to sea. We just looked at each other saying nothing and began to swim as hard as we could. We were surrounded by whitecaps and the ocean grew cold to our skin. We needed to get a bit closer to shore and we might free ourselves from this powerful slipstream. We were swimming for our lives and holding our breath at the same time. We finally made it to shore about a half mile down the coast, exhausted and scared, the rain came down in buckets. We packed our things and returned to New York.

Jon called me as soon as we got back and asked me to come to studio C, upstairs at the Record Plant because he and Jimmy needed to play something for me. When I arrived, Jimmy said, "This was the track that we were working on while you were out of town." "Oh no," said a little voice in my head. Trying to prepare myself for what I was about to hear, he added, "I just wanted to put some swing into it." His tone was tentative, borderline apologetic. They rolled tape.

My head exploded. What was once a rocking "balls to the wall" rendition of "Down in the Boondocks" had been reduced to a fucking "samba." The life had been completely sucked out of it. The clever treatment and arrangement of the song had not only been undermined, it was totally gone along with whatever artistic control that I had left. "We need you to do vocals," Jimmy said, with a completely straight face. I sat there and thought, "What makes these guys think that they can just leave me completely out of the creative process? Wasn't I the artist?" I then spoke up and argued, and I made it very clear that this was not a version of the song that I really wanted to put my name on.

Jimmy just reiterated about doing the vocals. The control room went silent; everybody stared at me. Under the duress of the moment I relented and sang the lead and did all of the background vocals. Apparently they needed an even bigger spoon to gouge my heart out so Jon called his old buddy Billy Joel to come in and do the background vocals over again thereby lending his name to the project. I suppose that I should have been impressed but I was still too pissed off. As previously mentioned, Jon and Billy had worked together before. Billy was riding high on his *Glass Houses* LP and Jon and Jimmy were desperately reaching for star power. There were no open tracks available for Billy so my pristine backing vocal tracks were erased. Billy showed up at the studio with some amount of cocaine, probably an eight ball. Everybody in the control room was getting high and I left the room because I couldn't bear to see what I knew was coming.

By the time that Billy decided to take on the background vocals at least two or three hours had slipped away. He was in no shape to sing, but sing he did. After all that partying it's not easy to get a good vocal tone, but Joel soldiered on.

This abomination was actually released later in 1980 on twelve-inch vinyl, which was an attempt to make a statement in and of itself, as it was big in size but unfortunately not very big of heart. Radio reports began filtering back from the field and the news wasn't good. Some found an abrasiveness about the record. No comments were actually specific, it seemed that no one was able to pinpoint the problem, but I believed I knew what it was. I can only speculate that the issue might have been the quality of Joel's voice when he added his harmonies. Having already made the attempt myself, I came to realize how difficult it can be to sing after doing a lot of blow. So what might have been a truly viable boost to the LP petered out to be next to nothing. I heard from someone that Jimmy was putting some of his own money into the single's promotion. If that's actually true, then it was either very generous or a feeble attempt on his part to save face. Unfortunately, whatever it was would be to no avail. This thing was dead, the album and subsequent single and very possibly my entire career.

At about midsummer, after "Boondocks" had officially been declared DOA, Clive put me on suspension. I still had a two album "firm" deal but this meant that he was stopping the clock on the contract. Arista's "mini-machine" that spun all things D. L. Byron would be shut down. The second record would only happen if Clive allowed it to. Of course, I had no idea that any of this could even happen, but just the same it was as though I was told to go sit in the corner and don the dunce cap. This was as distressing as it was humiliating. Why was I being punished because the record's sales didn't meet Arista's expectations? Maybe this company couldn't handle the diversity of its own roster. Would they send a promo guy to a radio station with my record in one hand and Barry Manilow's in the other? I simply didn't get it. I was pissed, and my world was crumbling.

It was always in moments of deep crisis like this when my mind would slip away to fantasizing about my real mother. If only I had her in my life. Maybe she could offer me a bit of wisdom and peace, as well as some much needed protection.

A few weeks went by and I got a call from Jimmy asking me to meet with him. At the time, as far as I was concerned he had brutally let me down, so I was very wary of any meeting. He had so cavalierly run roughshod over the whole process of producing my record, and then topped it off by creating a track that didn't even remotely represent me as an artist. I cautiously agreed to meet. We sat down on leather sofas in the lounge just adjacent the control room, and he began to tell me that he had just been made Music Coordinator for the upcoming Robert Stigwood film *Times Square*, which was being billed as sort of a punk *Saturday Night Fever*, the 1977 film that Stigwood had become so famous for. Jimmy wanted me to write an original song that would be the opening theme of the film. "It's your basic rich girl meets poor punk girl, they run away together and hide out in an abandoned pier on the Hudson. Then they begin sending cryptic messages to some late-night DJ," he explained. Tim Curry of *Rocky Horror Picture Show* fame was slated to play the DJ. I said that I would be happy to give it a try, thanked him, and went home and sat at the piano. I was still pretty numb at this point. I was guessing that Jimmy's gesture was coming from his own feeling of guilt for not having been there for the project. It felt like too little too late.

Within about twenty minutes I wrote "Shadows of the Night." It was one of those rare songs that simply wrote itself. I didn't labor over it, it simply appeared as soon as I was able to get out of its way. There are those times when writing a song can almost be a mystical experience. To simplify, it's when the writer is truly inspired rather than simply using the craft. At that particular moment I suppose you might say that I too felt very much like I was running through the shadows. I got permission to go up to Arista's office and use the small demo studio there and did a very simple piano/vocal. When I played it for Jimmy he seemed to like it and suggested that we do a full-blown demo to present to Stigwood. My regular drummer Thommy Price was busy with another project so I had to quickly find another drummer, a "heavy hitter." I called Gene Cornish who I knew from Fotomaker and asked him if he might ask his buddy, the great Dino Danelli, to play on the track. No one could speak directly to Dino, as he was too shy and reclusive, so I had to go through Gene. Dino agreed and showed up for the session and he couldn't have been nicer. He even took some suggestions from me as to how a certain drum phrase should appear in the chorus. The demo turned out sounding more like a record than your garden-variety demo. All the players were great, especially Dino. The drum sounds were huge, having intense power and a sense of drama, and this time Jimmy was actually there for the entire project, something I didn't really expect. He was pleased with the final product and submitted it for the film. I was feeling a glimmer of hope.

About a month or so had gone by when Jimmy called saying, "Hey, for whatever reason we just can't seem to fit "Shadows" into the film. I wanted it to be the opening theme but it's just not working." He then asked me to come to a session at another studio on Broadway where he was compiling the soundtrack. When I got there he played me a cassette of Graham Parker performing "You Can't Hurry Love" live in some British nightclub. This was the old Holland, Dozier and Holland song that was made famous by The Supremes. He looked at me and asked, "Do you think you could cop this?"

"Sure," I said, without any preconceived notion of how it would sound. I obliged and that's what finally made it into the film's soundtrack. *Times Square* had received quite a bit of hype and was opening at the Zeigfield Theatre in midtown. Opening night had all the glitz of a Hollywood premiere. I noticed Paul Simon chatting with Lou Reed along with many more notables walking around the well decorated lobby. Finally everyone took their seats and the theatre lights came down. From the very first scene this film was gut-wrenchingly awful. In the final cut, they actually left some incredibly blatant dialogue errors like, "I'm gonna brain your blows out," delivered by the film's female lead character, portrayed by Robin Johnson. Despite the film's innate horror, the soundtrack sold like crazy because everybody was on it—names like Patti Smith, Lou Reed, Talking Heads, XTC, The Pretenders, Roxy Music, and the Ramones made it the perfect party record. Unfortunately, Clive refused to sign the "Artist Release" for my appearance on that record. A month earlier, I had questioned him in a private meeting about how my record was handled. Like so many industry executives he could never be wrong and how dare I suggest otherwise. Over the following weekend someone snuck into the Arista building and took an axe to Clive's office doors. Those beautiful cherry hardwood double doors were hacked to pieces. I later heard gossip that he assumed that I was the culprit. I wasn't. Mr. Davis must have had real enemies. Nonetheless, I was never paid for my contribution to the soundtrack. Soon after, I hooked up with my old drummer Thommy Price. He had begun to record with Helen Schneider. She was an American artist who had a huge following in Germany. I gave him a cassette of the demo of "Shadows of the Night" and asked him to check it out.

In an interesting turn of events, Thommy Price played the demo of "Shadows" for Schneider and she decided to record it. It became the first single from her next album *Rock and Roll Gypsy* and was an instant multiplatinum hit in Germany and the Benelux countries. This initial "cover" of "Shadows" served me well in relegitimizing my talent, and my career.

Even though I was still on suspension at Arista I began submitting songs for my second record. When I submitted "Shadows of the Night," Clive's response was, "This isn't commercial enough". I thought that he was simply being vindictive. I knew in my gut it was a hit. Clive's "pass" on the song made me even more determined. I got a call from Rick Chertoff, Rachael Sweet's producer asking me to meet with them at the Record Plant once again in studio B. Sweet, who had been an artist for Stiff records, had landed a deal with Columbia. When I got there they expressed interest in doing the song, having heard Schneider's version, but Rachael wanted to change some of the lyrics and she also wanted half of the publishing. I told them that I would permit them to change whatever lyrics they liked, but I was not parting with any piece of the publishing and if that was a deal breaker, I didn't give a shit. "It's a huge hit in Germany . . . if you wanna cut it, fine . . . if not, fine!" I said walking out. That might have come off as angry, misplaced bravado but to my mind these were just another couple of industry weasels. Owning a copyright is like owning a house. You wouldn't let some stranger paint your house any color they like while you're away on vacation and upon your return claim partial ownership. She recorded it with some slightly rewritten rather banal lyrics posing as poetic. It was released and went nowhere.

I thought that I might look into shopping the song myself so I began to make some phone calls, one of which was to Jeff Aldridge an A&R exec that I knew at Chrysalis records, Pat Benatar's label. I brought a couple of versions of the song into the meeting suggesting that "Shadows" might work for Pat as it had for Helen Schneider. As far as pitching the song to Benatar, I suppose my thinking was that the song just might be better suited for a female vocal. In the meeting I mentioned that I wasn't interested in parting with a piece of the copyright and Jeff, whose industry nickname was "Buzzard," remained receptive but kind of gave me a "We'll see" kind of response.

Around that time I was finally falling out with my manager Jon Small. He and Judy Berger did very little to defend my position at Arista. My contract was still suspended, and Clive had passed on "Shadows", so I really had little interest in forging on with them at the helm. One day Jon called me to come over to his apartment for a chat. He lived on the upper East Side in a roomy two bedroom apartment that featured lots of mirrored walls. "You're basically out of money so you should probably go out and get a job," he said callously. Having foolishly allowed him to handle my finances, I assumed that what he told me was true. So I fired him. That may have been reckless but I was feeling completely ripped off and I was setting about to clear the deck of clutter. I felt betrayed by just about everyone. No one was standing up for me so I needed to stand up for myself. I was even becoming disenchanted with Laurie. Our relationship seemed to be crumbling and I told her that I wanted to live alone. Rather than offer me emotional support like one might expect from one's friends and family, she had begun to buy gold jewelry and go out to lunch every day with her friends. I had no support system. Stunned that I would dump her, instead of her dumping me, which would have been her original plan, she moved back to Hudson Street. A friend of hers was now living there and she would at least have a place to stay. I'd had it and I was cutting everybody loose.

I moved directly into the murky depths of drugs and alcohol. As 1980 became '81, I was severely depressed but didn't know it, and I fell into self-medicating. I was looking to fill a void in myself, an empty hole. It seemed to me that I had come such a long way, only to lose everything. I was threatened by everything and everyone. I was, in fact, actually shutting down.

One of my major "hang" bars was One University Place, located in the Village near NYU. It was owned and operated by Micky Ruskin who had once owned Max's Kansas City, probably the most renowned downtown restaurant and club during the early to mid-seventies. Max's was the home of Holly Woodlawn, Lou Reed, Todd Rundgren, and of course, Andy Warhol, whose factory was close by. Upstairs at the club you could catch bands like the New York Dolls and The Velvet Underground. Micky had sold Max's to the Dean family and it spiraled downward until eventually closing.

I had gone to One University one night to meet up with Jonathan Holtsman and a few of his friends, none of whom I knew. There were probably six people at our table including Des McAnuff, a theatrical director who would go on to win a

Tony for his direction of The Who's *Tommy*, and his soon-to-be-estranged wife and then-aspiring actress, Wendel Meldrum. They had just moved to New York from Toronto. She was a strikingly beautiful redhead that I was immediately attracted to. After some whispering in Jonathan's ear, he somehow got her to slip me her phone number under the table. Apparently she was as interested in me as I was in her. I pocketed the phone number but didn't call her for some time as I still had some "dogging around" to do. I just wasn't ready for a meaningful relationship. I would show up at various clubs like the Ritz or CBGB's and walk right in. Because of the record and live appearances around town, everybody knew who I was and I was able to pick up almost any girl that I cared to. One night I came home with a pair of twin sisters; my doorman thought I was a god. I was seeking self-validation through rampant promiscuity.

It was also around this time that something very strange began to happen. I was hearing a voice in my head. I couldn't always make it out but it was definitely there, and I don't mean to say that I was hearing voices, I was hearing only one voice and it was speaking directly to me. Years earlier while living on Bleecker Street, Laurie had given me a copy of *A Parenthesis in Eternity* by Joel S. Goldsmith. Throwing it into my lap she commanded me to read it or she would break up with me. She was always looking for any reason to break up with me then or even later by throwing me out of Hudson Street once or twice. I actually read the book and was impressed by its explanation of the laws of metaphysics. This later led me to begin buying books of an alternative nature. I started collecting books on parapsychology, comparative religions, the Kaballah, Rosicrucianism, Freemasonry, and various occult works including some written by members of the Order of the Golden Dawn such as Macgregor Mathers and Edward Arthur Waite. I bought even more books by Goldsmith, some by Krishamurti, as well as various Hermetica. I was buying just about everything that I could find, and still I could hear this voice talking to me. I bought a deck of tarot cards in hopes of developing my psychic ability. Weiser's bookstore on lower Broadway became my Mecca for all these books; they had everything you could want or ask for including antique collectible occult books locked in glass cases at the rear of the store.

I could still hear that voice; it wasn't clear or discernible but it was definitely speaking directly to me. I was either about to go completely crazy or surprisingly sane. One night after consuming some amount of vodka and cocaine I actually started to hear the voice much more clearly. You wouldn't think that would be the case but in fact, it was. It was suggesting that I get a pen and a pad of paper, which I did, then sitting down at my kitchen table I waited for more information. The voice instructed me to make a "pendulum" out of clear quartz crystal and some thread. For whatever reason, I had already begun to buy and collect various kinds of quartz and as it happened I found some thin nylon string hiding in a forgotten utility box in a closet. I attempted to wind the line around a piece of quartz and leave a long length on its end to create a pendulum. Next I was told to go to the kitchen and get a dish, not too big, something more like a lunch plate. I was then instructed to make what I later discovered was known as a planchette; of course I had no idea what a planchette was and had never even heard the term.

As I came to learn, this wasn't to be like the planchette of Ouija board fame, but rather a perfect circle with the letters of the alphabet arranged in a very particular order just outside of the circle. I traced a dish and began to put this all together.

I was also told to draw a "Star of David" inside the circle, taking up as much area as possible. Using a ruler I drew the star and suddenly we were speaking. I held the pendulum over the center of the circle and it began to spell out something. Quickly I grabbed my pad and began to transcribe what was being communicated. I watched as the pendulum swung from one letter to the next hitting each one twice as though for emphasis. G then to O then on to D, eventually spelling out the very first phrase, "God Goes With You." It started that simply but soon the floodgates seemed to open and I was writing furiously. Someone else might have resisted this unusual intervention but it just felt right to me. I stayed mostly awake for days writing down a slew of information that upon rereading, would prove to be more than astonishing. I was being told about past lives and what I was meant to do in this incarnation. Moreover, there were hints at the secrets of the universe and the voice was exhorting me to take up regular meditation. Sure I was depressed, up to my eyeballs in liquor and drugs, but I wasn't completely crazy, or at least, I didn't think so.

I continued with more questions for this entity or whatever it was. Eventually, I asked for its name. After a moment's pause, the pendulum spelled out I-P-R-U . . . IPRU. I heard it in my head as pronounced "EEPROO." I continued with more questions sometimes not even verbalizing them, just questions in my head. IPRU seemed happy to answer most things that I would ask. After what turned into a rather detailed and extensive Q & A session, I eventually got around to my birthmother. "Is my birthmother still alive?" I asked. Immediately the pendulum spelled out, "Yes."

"Would I actually find her one day?" I continued. Once again I received an immediate and resounding, "Yes." I finally felt a glimmer of hope that she might indeed be still alive. The terrible guilt that I had carried for so long for being responsible for her death might now begin to wane.

Just as it seemed as though this exchange might be winding down, there was a shift of some kind. Another entity wanted to speak. It identified itself as IGAU, "EEGOU." This came on very suddenly and with great power. I was told to put down the pendulum and simply listen. What happened next might be called automatic writing and it was profound. I began to simply transcribe whatever came into my head. I was writing what later seemed to be an invocation of some kind. The following is the first text that was dictated by IGAU:

WE ARE THE PRESENCE OF PURE BEING
THERE IS NO OTHER LIGHT THAN THAT OF THE LIVING GOD
OF WHICH WE ARE A DIVINE PART,
WE ARE NOW FULLY CONSCIOUS OF THE PRESENCE OF THE INDWELLING GOD.
WE NOW BEHOLD THE LIVING GOD. IN WHOSE LIVING IMAGE AND LIKENESS
WE ARE MADE.
JOYOUS IS OUR ASCENSION IN CONSCIOUSNESS WITHIN THE INFINITE SUPREME PRINCIPLE OF THE UNIVERSE
THAT PRINCIPLE WHICH HAS BROUGHT ALL LIFE INTO MANIFESTATION.
BORN OF LOVE AND LIFE ETERNAL.

I had never heard of anything like this happening to anyone. I suppose I thought that I was the only one, which made this spiritual tsunami all that much more dramatic and life changing. Eventually the thrust of this initial encounter wore down and I began to return to a more "normal" existence. It was almost impossible for me to openly share these experiences with anyone. Anytime I would attempt to share them with someone who was close to me, I would always get the "rolling eyes." As if to say, "Oh great, D. L. has completely lost his mind!" The memory of those days and nights stayed with me though, and I began to use the pendulum as a constant reference. It was like having a telephone to the other side. I've come to know these entities as my spirit guides or guardian angels. This arcane incident marked the beginning of a very long spiritual journey, a path toward self-realization that I am still on today. Although I no longer refer to my guides by name, as I eventually realized that names are inconsequential and only answer the mind's need for objectification. I can now hear them so well that I don't always need the pendulum. Maybe the words of the old sage are true, "There are many paths to the mountaintop but once there, the view is the same for all."

CHAPTER 15

BRINGING UP WENDEL

I sat staring at the tiny scrap of paper with her number on it somehow afraid to make the call. Calling a girl wasn't hard for me. I was a pro. But somehow this was different. Making this call meant something. A turning point, and by that I mean I had been hesitating because I felt that this might turn into a serious relationship and I wasn't entirely sure that was what I wanted. Although my escapades and indiscretions of late were wearing thin, somewhere inside I yearned for stability, for a sense of family, belonging. I didn't know if this girl would be the answer to that internal longing, but it sure was going to be a lot closer than the revolving door of women I currently called my life. "Hello?" she answered, not expecting me. "Hi, it's D. L., how are you?" I started. "What the hell happened to you? Every time any guy has called me for the past three months I thought it was you!" she snapped. Wendel was a very lighthearted woman who had a wonderful laugh. She was easy to talk to and be around. She could be very warm and empathetic and sometimes a bit dramatic but after all, she was an aspiring actress. She would eventually go on to play the "low talking" fashion designer

Leslie in *Seinfeld*'s 1993 "Puffy Shirt" episode. I had successfully freed myself of extraneous people. Anyone who was still standing in my universe approved. Everyone liked her.

The self-medicating continued and now for better or worse I had a new drinking buddy. Wendel was "pie-eyed," as she put it, most of the time. We began hanging out regularly. One day she got word that a friend of hers who lived in London had become terminally ill and had only a short time to live. She desperately wanted to see Wendel again, and after hearing of her impending divorce, had wished to introduce her to her friend Ray Davies of The Kinks.

As it happened, Wendel was losing her apartment in the East Village, and said to me that when (and if) she returned she would like to move in with me. I was being offered second place based on her romantic success with a former Kink? This situation had a particular smell and it wasn't floral. So, after just a few short months of dating, she went off to London for an undetermined amount of time and I was to simply stand by and see if I made the cut. This wasn't sitting very well with me but when she actually did return after seeing her friend and not hitting it off with Davies, the softie in me relented and she moved right in.

I was about to turn thirty and several months of our relationship had slipped by when she told me that she was pregnant. This came as quite a surprise to me because it was my understanding that she was on the pill. I didn't deal with this very well at all. With all that I had just been through the idea of parenthood scared the crap out of me. I was so confused and in my heart wasn't completely sure that Wendel was the one for me. If I was going to take on fatherhood I should have absolutely no doubt. Across the street in Abington Square we sat together on a park bench. In trying to talk it out she admitted that she too might not be ready. This was a very difficult decision but in the end we decided to terminate. It was a very sad time. When I got her home I did all that I could to make her comfortable hoping that this melancholy moment would eventually pass. This event impacted me greatly, in fact it slapped me into sobriety. I decided to stop drinking entirely and dry up for a while.

One sunny afternoon the phone rang, it was Jeff Aldridge calling me, the same A&R guy from Chrysalis that I had met with nine months earlier. "Well, I think that we finally got Pat to do the song but you need to agree to our terms," he said. Then came, "First of all, Pat would like to add some of her own lyrics." Naturally I was disappointed because Rachael Sweet had already done such a "hatchet job" on her version, yet something told me to hear him out. He already knew that I wouldn't part with a piece of the song. "We would also ask that you agree to a reduction on the mechanical rate," he continued. Simply put, I would be paid something less than the standard rate for each record sold. Normally this sort of arrangement would have been a deal breaker for me, but now we were talking about Benatar, who already had a couple of huge hits under her belt. Of course I didn't know at the time that the song was already "in the can" (recorded) and slated to be the first single from her new album *Get Nervous*. I verbally agreed to these terms, hung up the phone cordially and immediately called my attorney. "Fix this! Please . . . Do whatever you can!" He was able to negotiate with them a bit but what I was to be paid would still be below "statutory rate." I believed that my lawyer did the best that he could, given the situation, and I decided to live with it.

It seemed like the very next day that "Shadows of the Night" was all over the radio. I remember hearing it on air for the very first time. I was at home reading *Rolling Stone* magazine with the radio on. As I sat there reading I said to myself, "Hey . . . I know that song!" It was well produced and highly dramatic. I was impressed by the a cappella intro and the guitar solo was completely over the top. The reviews were excellent, sales were brisk, and the record was surely headed for multiplatinum status. The best part was that even after agreeing to a reduced pay rate I was still making some very serious money. The record hadn't been on the radio for much more than a few weeks when I got a call from Jon Small wanting to meet me for lunch. Although rather suspicious, I agreed to meet him at a restaurant in the Galleria building on 57th Street. Over lunch he expressed a keen interest in managing me again. The hairs on the back of my neck stood up. I thought that was very dark and suspect so politely, I declined his offer. The following week he sued me because I had written the song while still under contract with him. This was the same guy who who stood mutely by when Clive put me on suspension. In fact, years later I would discover that the Arista record was a hit in Spain and Australia. Jon never told me. No one did. I had written the song, I had secured the Benatar cover, and I was livid. Still having to defend myself from these shadowy snakes, my attorney was able to negotiate a settlement on my behalf which came with a sweet cash payout for Jon. In hindsight, it was worth every penny. Around the same time I asked my lawyer to get in touch with Arista and see if they would grant me a release. According to the label, I still owed them just under a quarter of a million in studio time that Jimmy had racked up. I had no other label to go to. Probably hoping to erase my memory, they agreed to release me. At the time I felt that if they had passed on "Shadows" then they had no clue about me or what I could offer. I was happy to move on. I felt like I was finally gaining some control over my life and career.

The Grammy Awards would be coming up soon, so I called around to ask if "Shadows" had been nominated for anything. "No, not to my knowledge," my attorney assured me. "Are you sure?" I pressed. "Nope, I haven't heard a thing," he said. So when Grammy night rolled around I said to Wendel, "Oh fuck it, let's just go out for dinner!"

"Are you crazy?" she cried. "This is your industry, you simply *have* to watch the awards!" I relented and we ordered in and sat on the couch watching the show. It was pretty much business as usual until they got to the "Best Female Rock Vocal" category. Benatar was in fact nominated. The very next minute, she had won and I watched as the camera panned over to an empty seat. "Pat is on tour so she will be unable to personally accept the award," said the host. Mostly elated but a bit miffed I stood up shouting at the TV, "I could have flown to L.A., accepted on her behalf as the writer, and let her chase me down for the fucking trophy."

Oddly enough, now that things seemed on track and moving forward I felt completely overwhelmed. In childhood, I was conditioned to fail so accepting this newfound success was difficult. I felt as though my feelings of abandonment by my birthmother had once again returned to haunt me. When moments of difficulty would arise, like when I was pressed to record vocals on a track that I knew was crap, I would easily relent or give in, instead of standing up for what I deserved and knew in my heart was right. Between all that had happened with Arista and given what was now going on with Pat's record, I was beginning to feel that I needed some time alone. Looking back at all the years of "brick walls," "hurry up and wait," and the occasional "near miss" all thrown in together with my inevitable associations with back-alley thieves and industry weasels, I began to wonder how I attracted all these things into my life in the first place. I wanted so much to be accepted and loved, yet I surrounded myself with people and situations which only served to do the opposite. Somehow, I had managed to create exactly the reality that I didn't want. Why was I cutting my own throat? Why did I insist that I didn't deserve happiness or success. Even though I now had so much to be grateful for, somehow I was still filled with fear. I was pretty much on the verge of a breakdown.

After the pregnancy, my relationship with Wendel never really recovered. She wasn't actively looking for auditions so her professional aspirations had been temporarily thwarted. She had become very needy, looking to me to divert attention away from her own plight. It all just felt like a giant weight around my neck. So I informed her that I would find an apartment for her, pay for the first month or two, but she needed to move out. This wasn't easy as she was pretty firmly entrenched in my place. I wasn't really looking for an actual breakup but I needed space. I found her a nice apartment, even bought her some furniture, and thought that I would leave New York for the summer. Just as I was preparing to go I got a call from a girl that I saw occasionally when I was still bar hopping. She told me that one of her clients was selling the lease to his loft. This was commonly known as a "fixture fee" deal and was probably one of the last to be had on the island of Manhattan. It was an entire third floor of a three-story building on Grand Street in Chinatown. The lease was assignable for a price and it was held by Chris Parker, a jazz drummer of considerable renown. She put Chris and I together and we made a deal. For eleven thousand dollars I would take over his lease and my rent would be less than half of what I was paying on Abington Square. I jumped on it, paid the fixture fee, moved in all of my belongings, and locked the door behind me. I now had a new place to come back to in the fall. I was ready to leave for the summer and more than ready to forget about everything and everyone.

CHAPTER 16

MYSTERY GIRL

Being from South Jersey I decided to rent an apartment for all of July and August in historic Cape May, a beautiful town at the southernmost tip. This turned out to be exactly what I needed. I rented a two bedroom apartment in a lovely old Victorian house just a block from the beach. I had no trouble finding companionship, especially with a gigantic hit all over the radio. Wendel would take the bus down from time to time. I was lying on the beach one afternoon and noticed a strikingly beautiful girl sitting on a towel not too far away from me. She wore a secondhand white tuxedo shirt over her swimsuit to protect her from the sun. She was tall and blonde but I just couldn't get up the nerve to go up to her and introduce myself. Normally this would not have been a problem for me but somehow this girl was different. The very next day there she was again, and again the day after. This was beginning to drive me a little crazy. Cape May has miles of beaches so why was she turning up at mine? Did she live nearby? Was she just here for the summer? I couldn't get her out of my head.

Maybe being so close to my hometown made me nostalgic. Maybe I felt an urge to be in touch with family, such as it was. I decided to reach out to my father and ask if he and his wife would join me for dinner in Cape May. He had remarried a few years back and his new wife systematically began separating him from his entire family. I was the first to go, not being invited to his wedding, or even being notified that he married. For whatever reason I felt willing to try to put all of that behind me. I made the call. He agreed, so he and his wife, Gertrude, came and met me at my apartment, then we walked over to West Cape May for a nice dinner at McGlades, which had become a favorite eatery of mine. They served good home-style Italian cuisine and had the best dinner rolls. A bit pricey, but nothing was too good for my deadbeat absentee dad. We sat down and the waitress brought a basket of rolls, only this time they were hot dog buns. I called the waitress over and not even looking at her I simply said, "I know you have great dinner rolls here, could you please take these buns back?" She nervously explained that the McGlade family had a barbecue earlier that day and the restaurant was trying to get rid of the buns. She apologized and took them away. I was so nervous about seeing my father again and meeting his new wife that I failed to realize that our waitress was the mystery girl from the beach. When I finally recognized her that was it. I had no recollection of anything that was said during dinner save to say that I really didn't care for Trudy, as she liked to be called. Trudy came off to me as being shallow and controlling. Anytime my father tried to speak she interrupted him and began to talk about herself. I wasn't impressed. I could only think about this girl.

Dinner came to an end, I paid the bill and said goodbye to my father and his new wife. When I got back to my apartment

I looked in my wallet and realized that I hardly had any cash left. What the hell did I do? Had I made a mistake of some kind? So I went back to the restaurant looking for an answer.

I confronted our gorgeous waitress and asked her to pull the bill. She quickly obliged and I realized I had mindlessly given her a $60 tip on a $110 dinner. I was terribly embarrassed and sheepishly said, "I hope you don't think that I want anything of the tip back; it was completely my mistake and if you ever see me in town sometime I would be happy to buy you a drink!" She laughed nervously saying, "Sure no problem." What an ass I had been, and on top of that, I still couldn't muster up enough nerve to ask her out.

Along the main drag in Cape May there was a stream of bars and restaurants, and one of the more popular places was called "Gloria's." I wandered in there one night about a week after the restaurant scene, thinking that I might just do some people watching and have a drink. It was a large open room, the kind of bar where you could just relax or you could get up and dance to whatever the DJ was playing. When I sat down I remember hearing Talking Heads. I wasn't much of the dancing type, at least that night I really wasn't in the mood. I was still brooding about having seen my father and how he had married some controlling bitch when I began to realize the similarities between Trudy and my mother. He needed someone to take care of him, to boss him around and keep him in line, otherwise he would be lost. My mother had done that for him and now Trudy would do the same. He had exactly what he needed. He was not capable of more.

I felt a little tap on my shoulder. I turned around and it was her, the mystery girl, who immediately said, "I think you owe me a drink." I asked for her name; "Leslie," she said. "I'm David . . . so what are you drinking?"

"I'll have a Rolling Rock," she said, taking the stool next to mine. We began to casually chitchat when some guy walked over and tapped her on the shoulder, asking her to dance, and off she went. "Oh fucking great!" I thought, but after a few minutes she was back. We had another round and I asked if she wanted to take a walk on the beach and maybe go back to my apartment and talk. This wasn't my usual sexual ploy. I really wanted to know all about this girl and I definitely did not want her to know anything about me, at least not just yet. I had become more than wary of people treating me a certain way, or trying to impress or ingratiate themselves to me simply because of who I was or what I had going on. If there would be any sex at all, it would have to be after I had gotten to know her. I needed to find out who this beautiful girl really was. There would be plenty of time for *my* complicated story later.

We got back to my place and I simply began to ask her about herself, what kind of music she liked, what were her aspirations. She told me that she really liked Cat Stevens, James Taylor, and had recently gotten into the Alan Parsons Project. "This is good . . . soft rock . . . but okay," I thought to myself. "I'm studying architectural engineering at Penn State, it's a five year program. I've got two years left to go," she added. When she graduated she wanted to design and build things, big things. We talked for hours and somehow I managed to stay off the "me" topic. Before we realized, it was four thirty in the morning. I offered to walk her home; the old Victorian cast iron street lamps lit our way. We exchanged phone numbers and that was it for the night.

Back then I was driving a baby blue 1965 Ford Mustang three-speed. I bought it the year before in Vineland when I was down visiting Aunt Marie. I got this classic car for a great price because it needed a bit of work under the hood. In West Cape May I had found a mechanic who did quality work for a reasonable price. Leslie and I became a regular thing, driving that Mustang all over the Jersey Shore. We couldn't get enough of each other, becoming practically inseparable. Being with her on an almost daily basis was transforming my entire state of mind. My heart was ready. The only loose end was that I hadn't officially broken up with Wendel yet. I had gotten her out of my apartment and she would visit me from time to time, but now that had to change. I was speaking to her on the phone one afternoon when I noticed that someone was slipping something under my apartment door. I quickly finished up the phone call and retrieved the package. It was a copy of the new Police album *Synchronicity*. I ran to the window to see that Leslie was already almost out of sight. I was actually falling in love for the first time in my life and I wanted nothing to jeopardize it. Something had always told me that I would never find my mate in New York City. She had to be from somewhere else, not my hometown either but somewhere else, and I was sure that she was the one.

By this time she had learned all about me, and naturally her friends were very impressed that she was dating an alleged rock star (and I use that term very loosely), but I still didn't want any of that to weigh in too heavily. I wanted her to love me for me.

During my phone conversation with Wendel, she said that she really wanted to see me face to face, so I thought that I would be a man and drive to New York and tell her that it was over. When she answered her apartment door she was struggling to get a shirt pulled over her bare chest. I guessed that might have been a last-ditch effort to try to entice me. It didn't work. I told her to go ahead and see other people, wishing her the best. I didn't even think to stop and check on my new apartment, I just got back in the Mustang and headed for South Jersey.

Upon my return I told Leslie what had happened. I knew that as the summer drew to an end she would be heading back to school and I would be back in New York. I really wanted to be sure that our relationship was firmly cemented. This girl was driven and very much her own person, but at the same time so caring and empathetic. I had never met such a fascinating woman. I had fallen in love with her and I wanted her to know exactly how I felt. Her mother, Joan, was coming from Lansdale, PA, to pick her up to take her home. We said a long goodbye and I promised her that she wouldn't easily be rid of me. I was already planning to start visiting her at Penn State. She later told me that all the way home she kept telling her mother about this really unique guy that she had met and that she felt a very serious bond.

At summer's end I returned to New York to begin putting my apartment and my life back together. I continued having bouts of depression but still didn't realize what my problem was.

Then one morning, my car disappeared. I had parked the Mustang on Chrystie Street just around the corner from the new loft. I went down to get it and it was gone. Stolen. I filed a police report, and the officer noting the make and model sarcastically said, "Well, you're never gonna see *that* car again." Cars would simply vanish only to reappear at any number of "chop shops" in Brooklyn. That Mustang was worth more in pieces than it was whole.

I went down to visit Aunt Marie for a few days. I hadn't seen her since the beginning of the summer and it was a good time to catch up, and I could tell her all about Leslie. I could also ask her to accompany me once again to go car shopping. When I walked in her back door she was sitting at the kitchen table as she always did. She put down her coffee and snuffed out her Virginia Slim and gave me a big hug. She looked good, still all piss and vinegar, and all too happy to help me look for another car. Together we hit the usual auto lots along Delsea Drive in Vineland.

Buying a car down in South Jersey was always a pretty good bet. It was actually possible to find something decent with low mileage. We came across a 1977 Datsun 280 Z. This was a really cool sports car and the very same make and model that Paul Newman had made famous when he was racing.

I now had the perfect vehicle for the five hundred mile round-trip to State College, Pennsylvania, the home of Penn State University and Leslie. So what began as every other weekend quickly escalated to every weekend. In fact sometimes I would drive out just to pick her up and take her back to the city for the weekend. It was Route 80 all the way from Penn State to New York City, and every once in a while I could really open that Z car up. We would zip right through straightaways sometimes reaching speeds of nearly 150 mph. Leslie was very helpful in putting my loft together, plus I got to show her around the city, which was cool because "Shadows" was still on the radio and I could still just walk into any club.

As I was now officially moved into my loft on Grand Street, I decided that I needed a pet. I went out and bought a parrot, a Blue Front Amazon. Since I was living in Chinatown I named her Ming, after "Ming the Merciless" from the old *Flash Gordon* series. I used to walk with her on my shoulder through the city streets; she would sit on a bandana which caught the poop. She went everywhere with me, even making the long drives to Penn State.

Leslie's roommates made a semi-permanent perch for Ming. Creatively using some pieces of wood, a shoe box, and a plastic aquarium palm tree, they created what they called "Ming's Green Parrot Lounge." Secured to an entry railing, Ming had a place to sit in the living room where all the action was.

I had just turned thirty, it was 1983 and New York was enjoying an unusual kind of renaissance. There were lots of clubs to check out, great out-of-the-way restaurants, and of course, a mountain of cocaine the size of Everest. On any given night you would see someone walking around the East Village looking like they had just snorted a box of Entemann's powdered donuts. We would go to the Limelight or Danceteria, CBGB's was still happening, and there were countless other places. I did, however, have some other much more pressing issues to work out.

It appeared as though some of the professionals who were working on my behalf during the Arista days seemed to have been less than responsible with money. My CPA at the time, who worked hand in hand with Jon, had more than one set of books cooking and at the end of 1980 told me that I owed the IRS more than fifty thousand dollars. This was an amount of money that I simply didn't have on hand, as so much had somehow mysteriously disappeared. He suggested that I not file at all. That was terrible advice, and I wound up not filing for a few years as a result. So I had some legal crap, financial crap, and some serious tax crap to deal with.

As it turned out, Leslie, a banker's daughter, was very good with stuff like this. Once she figured out what was actually going on, I found a tax attorney to help me solve my problems with the IRS. I couldn't sue anyone because of a no-action clause which seemed insurmountable. So I was left to simply deal with it as best as I could. It was bad . . . very bad . . . but at least for the very first time in my life I was in love as well as having unconditional support. When she touched my hand something traveled right through me.

Leslie's parents, Web and Joan Haag, didn't care very much for me. Her father was in finance and her mother was a former kindergarten teacher. They had never met anyone like me so naturally I filled them with shitless fear. Apparently both familiarity and unfamiliarity manage to breed contempt. I suppose me showing up at their house with a parrot on my shoulder like some fucking pirate didn't help too much either. They couldn't understand how a songwriter could possibly make any money. They naturally assumed that I was broke and just mooching off of their only daughter, and seized every possible opportunity to let me know exactly what they thought. It got so bad that when we would drive down to Lansdale, Pennsylvania, for a weekend I found myself getting physically sick and on the verge of throwing up from the tension. Leslie had a really difficult time standing up to her parents, but eventually she did. In the midst of an argument she cautioned them not to ask her to choose between them and me. When she told me about it I felt grateful and also reassured that I had chosen well.

I had a friend named Jack that rented a small fishing shack every Summer out in Sag Harbor on Long Island. He would let me go there when he was otherwise busy for the weekend. It was now summer of '84 and I was planning to take Leslie there for several days, and told her parents of our intentions. Leslie's mom started going on about Leslie having just had some minor oral surgery, trying to claim that a weekend away would be too risky. I was trying to eat a sandwich in the kitchen and her mother began to storm in and out of the room in a huff but saying nothing. She looked like she was dressed for church, or maybe just an afternoon out, and the click of her heels behind me sounded like a message being sent in Morse code from an angry five year old. Finally I looked up at her and asked, "Do you actually think that I couldn't take care of her if something should go wrong?" Her father was standing in the doorway hearing all of this and a very slight smile came to his face. No one ever stood up to this woman. When she behaved like a spoiled child, everyone around her just allowed it. I wasn't about to cave.

I took Leslie to Sag Harbor that weekend with some friends from the city and we all had a great time. Along for the ride were Randy Rolin and his new wife, Carla. We all pitched in and made a makeshift perch for Ming out of branches we found near the beach. She sat outside of the shack all day just watching us swim. As mentioned, Randy had something of a coke business on the side so there was no shortage of partying. Just the same there was nothing otherwise nefarious about the weekend, only the lasting image burned into my brain of a rather overweight Randy sitting on the bow of a tiny Sunfish, looking like Ed Asner in Speedos, trying to figure out why the boat wasn't moving.

After a year of trying I got on slightly better terms with Joan and Web, good enough in fact that I was able to call Joan and ask for her help. I wanted to propose to Leslie, and hopeless romantic that I was, I wanted to do it on horseback. I suppose I thought that proposing that way would add a nice cinematic touch. I asked her if she might know someone who could rent me a horse for a couple of hours on Christmas Day. In fact she was able to find someone and promised to make the arrangements, as it was now clear that I wished to marry her daughter. My only problem was a ring. I was between royalty payments and didn't have quite enough for the kind of ring that I wanted. I drove down to visit Aunt Marie and took her out for dinner. I had already brought Leslie to meet Aunt Marie in fact we had spent weekends with her so I knew that she approved. I was just beginning to explain my dilemma when she took the ring from her finger and put it in my hand saying, "Honey . . . give her this. It was your mother's." I was dumbstruck by her thoughtful generosity. Apparently the diamonds in this ring were all Russian and were part of another ring that at one time had at its center a large marquis. My mother and Marie would often exchange items, borrowing them from each other for a while but they would always return them. My mother must have loaned Aunt Marie the ring in one of those exchanges, maybe just before her passing. Aunt Marie had somehow lost the large diamond so she had the others reset in white gold. I hugged and kissed her, asking for her blessings.

On Christmas morning, filled with anticipation, I drove off to Lansdale. As I drove over the Walt Whitman bridge leading from Jersey to Pennsylvania, I actually yelled to the toll taker, "I'm getting engaged today!" When I pulled up to the house I saw a man sitting in a horse drawn cart about a block away. This was my man. He unhitched one of the horses, saddled it up, and wished me luck. As planned, Leslie's entire family, her parents and brothers and others were sitting in the family room. I began to circle the house trying to get someone's attention. Her brother Dave saw me and just gave me an under wave, acknowledging me but pretending not to see me. The horse just wanted to circle the house, and I couldn't figure out how to get it to stop.

"Wait . . . Hey!" I shouted, "this horse won't stop!" Nobody heard me. For a second, I flashed back to riding "Peanut" at Oz's family farm in Jersey during my Peddie days. Horses and

I really didn't have a fabulous history. I really just needed to figure out a way to get this animal to stop at the front door, get off and ring the doorbell, and quickly get back on the horse before it wandered off. Somehow I managed and Leslie came to the door. She was really surprised but said that she had to change into jeans because she might ruin her stockings. So the horse and I just stood there waiting, risking the complete loss of any possible moment of romance. Finally she came back out and I helped her get on the back of the horse. There was a big open field just across the street so I headed for it. In the middle of a clearing I pulled the ring box from my breast pocket, passed it back to Leslie, and asked her to marry me. She said, "Yes!" By the horse's behavior, I think that he might have had a girlfriend nearby. He just wanted to roam in a different direction than I did. We trotted for a bit through the field that would later be sold off and developed into cookie cutter houses. I returned the trusty steed to the carriage man. It was Christmas and this had been very romantic after all. Leslie would be graduating in the spring and so we planned our wedding to take place in Leslie's hometown on September 22, 1985. I would be thirty-two and Leslie twenty-three years old.

She was determined to make not only her own wedding gown, a rather ornate and complicated garment to be sure, but also all the bridesmaids' gowns as well. Leslie had actually won the "Pearl S. Buck Award" for sewing when she was seventeen. She asked me to hand paint the bridesmaids' shoes with fabric paint to match their dresses. If she had more time she would have built a church. I had arranged for more conventional rental tuxedos for myself and my party.

I think that Leslie's parents, who lived in a modest three-bedroom suburban rancher, saw this as an opportunity to throw a huge party to impress their friends. I think that Joan thought, or maybe had hoped, that our marriage would last no more than two years. She convinced Leslie not to inscribe the silver, telling her to wait and see. I invited all of my friends, which included every musician I knew and most of my family. I did make the mistake of asking Jonathan Holtsman to be my best man. He was divorced from his wife Tina, and when he found out that I had invited her to the wedding, he threatened to pull out at the last minute. He seemed to forget the fact that I was best man at his recent wedding to his second wife, and he had invited Laurie, my ex, and her new boyfriend. I should have let him back out, he was being a dick, but instead I actually called Tina to uninvite her. This was so wrong and I felt terrible doing it. Ed Dondero, my old and dear friend from first grade, should have stood with me. I regret to this day not having asked him. Jonathan had become my best "city friend" but after the way he behaved I should have let him walk. I even invited my father and Trudy, why, I'm still not sure. Of course Aunt Marie was there, as well as her older nephew Vincent and his wife, Grace, so she would have familiar company around her.

The morning of the wedding something was brewing at the hotel. For one thing I forgot to pack socks so Leslie's father, still not completely sure about me, drove over with a pair just as I was about to spray paint my ankles black. I got the feeling that there was something going on between my father and Aunt Marie. This didn't surprise me, and although the nature of the scuffle was kept from me, I still sensed it might be serious. After the ceremony we were taking some group pictures in the church when Ed ran in saying that my father was leaving. I ran out to catch him and he said that they would be right back, but he and Trudy got into their car and sped off in a cloud of dust. Had something happened in the receiving line? What the hell? Now there would be two empty seats at the dais. I was distressed and stunned. I later found out from Aunt Marie that one of the things that Trudy was upset about was my name change. I had it legally changed back in 1979 and was proud that Leslie would take it. Marie told me that according to Trudy no one actually changed their name in show business, at least not legally. As though she might actually be an authority on such things. She had fully expected my last name to still be Mesiano. I wondered if she even knew that I was adopted.

A classic 1960 grey Bentley had been rented to take us to the reception, which was being held at a country club in Norristown, PA. Imagine a reception hall filled with nearly two hundred somewhat bigoted and anti-Semitic Protestants drinking scotch and rye, making comments about people they didn't know but thought were utterly distasteful and looked terribly strange. Most bathroom stalls had three to four people crammed inside doing blow. My old drummer Thommy Price was there; he was now playing with Billy Idol and the place was all abuzz about that. The biggest disappointment was the band that we chose. They were fine until it came time for our wedding song, "Every Step You Take" by the Police. That was the monstrous hit song from their *Synchronicity* LP, the very same record that Leslie had slipped under my apartment door just after we first met. I would have preferred the song be sung by Ethel Merman rather than these guys. In one, albeit brief, moment of calm, I sat down at the piano with my lovely new bride in her flowing gown and veil and sang a song entitled "Crazy," which I wrote with Benny. "I've seen a lot of people, and hear a lot of talk. But I don't let it get to me . . . and it's kinda hard when you love someone, haven't you been in my shoes, don't you know what it's like to lose . . . and I'm Crazy, I'm Crazy . . . oh I'm Crazy and I'm lost without you." People were coming up to me with teary eyes saying it was the best wedding ever. Benny, however, was a complete no-show. I had rented a tux and shoes for him but he never even called. Later I learned that a mutual friend, Bill McGathy who worked in radio promotion, had mistakenly told him that the wedding was in the middle of Pennsylvania, halfway to Ohio. Or in other words, he thought it was at Penn State when in reality it was held just outside of Philadelphia. So both Bill and Benny blew it off. I wasn't that surprised. Benny had always been pretty much "Mr. One Way". Besides I was much more hurt and sufficiently embarrassed by my own father's disappearance. Pretty soon it was over and we were being driven to New York to catch a flight to Jamaica.

CHAPTER 17

LITTLE LOFT ON THE PRAIRIE

The first morning of our honeymoon, we drove up to the cliffs outside of Negril. The trees were slow dancing and the air smelled like fresh coconut. I told Leslie to leave me off at the bottom of the hill, take the car to the top, and pull over. I had been to this place years before with my bass player Joe Vasta, so I remembered a row of little shanty shacks before the cliffs that sold mushrooms. I treaded down to this old familiar place, not much had changed over the years. After securing a small purchase, I put them in my shorts pocket and started up the hill. About halfway up I stopped in my tracks. A policeman standing next to our rental car was talking to Leslie. I panicked. He would know what I had been up to so I poked a hole in my pocket and began to drop the mushrooms out of my pants. He was watching me closely. I still had a few when I reached the car. "What's in your hand, Mon?" asked the officer. "Mushrooms sir," I replied. "You know they are illegal here!" he said with a crooked smile. "What?" I exclaimed, "I was going to put them in a salad!" He asked where we were staying and said he would be by to check on us later. "Oh bloody hell," I said under my breath, "turn the car around and let's get the fuck out of here." I quickly shoved what remained in my hand into my mouth and ate them all just to get rid of the evidence.

We stayed at a lovely place called Crystal Waters which was right on the ocean. This private compound with its own white sand beach offered cozy bungalows with a private cook, Myrna, who made breakfast and prepared dinner, leaving it in the oven for us to heat up when we returned from the beach. Our first day was just total relaxation. Leslie and I smoked some local Ganja and of course I was tripping quite well, thank you. Shrooms always seemed like more of a physical high to me but of course, you still trip your ass off.

At five o'clock a police car pulled in with two men inside. Both men got out of the car as we were coming up from the beach and I recognized the uniformed officer from that morning. He had a man in plain clothes with him. I asked them to come inside and have a drink, they agreed, and before I knew it they had smoked all my cigarettes and finished off all the beer. We made some small talk about me buying real estate there, I gave them twenty bucks, and they were off. I stood waving goodbye as they pulled down the driveway. "Well that could have been much worse," I thought. That's the only real drawback about Jamaica, being constantly hassled. You could be dead asleep on the beach and someone would wake you up to try to sell you something. These officers of the law were no different, just taking advantage of tourists wherever they could. The beautiful thing about Negril was going to Rick's Cafe on the cliffs at sunset. You could dive off the cliff into the gentle waters below, holding your breath long enough to touch the bronze statue of the Virgin Mary at the bottom of the inlet. Then you'd come back to the surface, climb the rope ladder up the cliff, and do it all over again.

At the end of the week we returned to the lawless Wild Wild West that was Chinatown and "The Little Loft on the Prairie," our third floor walk-up on Grand Street. I had the entire floor of a tenement building that was more than a hundred years old. This place was Lower Eastside chic. It was spacious and had tons of "old world" charm. Some of the plaster walls in the loft still had the original ornamental metal stamping, recalling the designs of old tin ceilings. Out on the street, the Bowery was still what it had always been, flophouses, nasty bars, hookers, and heroin.

One very big upside was our downstairs neighbor Michael Brecker, probably one of the best alto tenor sax players ever. He had established himself as quite the "jazz god," and played in the band on SNL. He was a very sweet and generous guy who had recently cleaned up from a pretty bad heroin habit. He was always a pleasure to be around. The only sticking point about having Michael as a neighbor was that the thermostat for both our floors happened to be in his apartment. He would crank up the heat so high that it was actually difficult to get out of bed in the morning. I was so warm and toasty in my sweaty sheets that I just wanted to keep on sleeping. Finally I confronted him. "Michael, are you really that cold? Do you really need to turn the heat up that much?" I asked, somewhat confounded. "It's not me, man, my horns like the heat," he said and laughed. It didn't occur to me until years later that ex-junkies are also cold all the time.

Ming was back from the "bird sitter." She loved the new Mexican wrought iron cage I bought for her. That thing was like a duplex for a small bird. Parrots become very attached to their owners so at first, Ming was jealous of my new bride being in "her space." Once we got ourselves settled in everything began to run smoothly. Leslie was interviewing for construction management positions and finally landed one. Soon she was running a project, building condos on Chambers Street. But she really had her eye on somehow getting into fashion design. God knows she could sew.

One weekend we thought that it might be nice to drive Aunt Marie up to New York and have her stay with us for a few days. She was in pretty good health, although she still smoked and had some trouble getting up the stairs, so once inside she camped out on the couch. I woke up in the middle of the night to find her awake and staring out the window. I gently asked, "Are you okay? It's really late you know." She claimed she hadn't been able to sleep because she was too busy watching the hookers down on the corner. "There's a big black girl with a huge chest but no one is stopping for her, poor thing," she said. She was looking at "DeeDee." I had gotten her coffee a couple of times because the late night Chinese bakery refused to serve the ladies. Coming from South Jersey my dear aunt had never seen anything quite like this. After a few days of hooker watching I drove Aunt Marie home.

I was making the adjustment to married life, trying to stay positive, still fighting depression. Leslie's dream of becoming a fashion designer began to take shape. She started to attend Parsons and later FIT (Fashion Institute of Technology) at night. I had no publisher at the time which meant no one was pitching my material. Just the same, I kept writing and recording in my home studio. Despite my efforts, I began suspecting that I was slipping even deeper into darkness. I had recently heard that depression could be genetic, but because of my adoptive status I couldn't point to a family link. Still I wondered if I was predisposed. And would I actually get a solid answer to that question one day? My drinking was once again accelerating and I had begun hanging out at Randy's apartment on 16th Street so I would have open access to cocaine. From the entry door of Randy's apartment, I would pass through a dingy narrow hallway toward his living room where on any given night the famous and the infamous of the music, television, and advertising world would be huddled around his coffee table passing the straw. The cramped living room of Randy's nocturnal grotto had but one window which looked out to a shaft way. Nobody ever knew what time it was and as long as there was blow on the coffee table, nobody cared. We dispersed at sunrise only to repeat the same debauchery the following night. Randy was something of a social vampire, attempting to elevate himself by thinking that his clients actually stayed around because they were hypnotized by his personality. He was in fact simply trying to suck them down to his level. As misery loves company, I was quite miserable enough to seek out his company on a fairly regular basis, at least a few times a week. Finally, he called me one night saying that he needed to come over and see me. "I gotta get outta here, man," he said in a panic.

I told him to come right over. His wife Carla had left him months before and he had hooked up with someone else. When he got to my place he plopped down into a chair in the living room and blurted, "The guys came to my door. . . I have to get out of town!"

"What guys?" I asked.

"The fucking Colombians, man, they came to my door . . . they had fucking guns! They want their money tomorrow or I'm totally fucked, man . . . I grabbed my stash and dumped it in a can across the street!" What I was almost certain would eventually happen to Benny was instead happening to Randy.

I wasn't sure if he was hallucinating or not as he nodded off in the chair obviously having been awake for days. Once I was sure that Randy was unconscious, I got an old beat-up coat from the closet and set about trying to make myself look as disheveled and homeless as I possibly could. I put on an old crumpled hat and some work boots that I should have tossed years before and made my way over to 16th Street. Once I got to his block, I put on the "homeless" show, walking crooked and even dragging my right leg a bit. I opened up each trash can one by one, slamming down the lids so people would think that I was drunk and dangerous. Then suddenly voila, I had found it. Appearing as if encircled by a silver halo was nearly an ounce of pure Colombian cocaine which I quickly put in my pocket. The next morning I got Randy up and put him into a cab. I never saw him again. Weeks later I heard he had abandoned his apartment on 16th Street, walked out the door with just some clothes in a bag, and fled to his sister's place in Virginia. That was the end of Randy. And once I had finished off his stash, mercifully, it was also the end of my romance with cocaine. He was gone and I was done.

I was still binge drinking as a means to manage my depression. Although at times I would have spells of lucidity when I would snap out of it and become quite productive. It was during one of those periods that I thought to reach out to Catholic Charities and resume the search for my birthmother. I had contacted the Archdiocese of Camden years before only to be told that they wouldn't help. It's difficult to explain but even though I truly wanted to find her, I felt so terribly guilty. I sat staring out my living room window down at the busy street below and imagined to myself just how threatened my adoptive mother would have been if I openly expressed my desire. After all, she went so far as to tell me that my real mother was dead; that's worth about least two years on some shrink's couch. Suddenly it came back to me, "Didn't she once tell me that my birthmother had red hair and freckles just like I did? How could she know that if they had never met?" Then my thoughts turned to Aunt Marie. "What would she think?" I wondered. "Would she approve or would she protect her sister?" In the end, I just said to myself, "Aw fuck it," and decided right then and there to proceed. At that time the Archdiocese of Camden had done a full reversal on their stance in helping adoptees find their blood. They assigned me a caseworker whose name was Betty. She was semi-retired and worked out of the Camden office. I felt a bit awkward as we spoke on the phone for the first time, but I quickly sensed her gentle nature. "I just love my part-time job. I love helping people find their real families," she said softly. "Plus I get to play golf twice a week!" That brief conversation did much to put my mind at ease and I did not feel so completely riddled with guilt. She took on my case, assuring me that she would do her best, but very soon the entire issue was put on hold because Aunt Marie was having some difficulties getting along. She was now in her late seventies and things were catching up. She lived a fairly sedentary lifestyle, only moving from the kitchen table to the couch. Her health had begun to falter with a mild heart condition and poor circulation. She could still get around the house by herself, but little else. Leslie and I drove down there on weekends, slept on the floor, bought her groceries, and tried to help her to keep herself and the house together. Sometimes on a Friday night when we arrived I might say, "Aunt Marie! We're gonna take you to the beauty parlor tomorrow." We would wake up the next morning to find her fully dressed to impress as she used a mirror to put the finishing touches on her eyebrows. They were usually painted slightly above her real ones. Afterward we would sometimes go out for dinner. She loved to be wined and dined. At heart, Marie was still a party girl.

My uncle Tony had two nephews, and one of them, Gene, and his wife, Gloria, were very nice to me and appreciated what I was trying to do for Marie. Vincent, the older nephew and his wife, Grace, were quite the opposite. The latter couple would appear at will and openly criticize everything I was doing and would go out of their way to make things difficult for me. I speculated that they were affronted by the trust that Aunt Marie seemed to place in me. Or maybe they just weren't very nice people.

Aunt Marie had a tenant, a middle-aged Russian woman named Rosa who had lived upstairs for years paying very little rent. When I was very young, Vincent had lived on the second floor of the house with his sister Marion, who I called Aunt Bebe. She was rather well endowed and I must confess that I would make repeated attempts at playing with her bosom. He wasn't often there as he had enrolled in a seminary with the intention of entering the priesthood. I do remember watching Vincent shaving one morning. He looked at himself so sternly as he applied bits of toilet paper to his razor cuts. It was while he was a seminarian that he met Grace, who was in a convent preparing to become a nun. They eventually left their respective vocations behind to be with each other and start a family, but they brought with them a virtual boatload of guilt and shame. They were very judgmental and utterly insufferable, plus they were very jealous of my relationship with my aunt and made no attempt to hide it. They had felt that I had abandoned Aunt Marie when I moved to New York or at least that's the rationale they used to assert their deservedness of her affection, her money, and her house. In many ways they acted as my parents had. They were unsupportive, cold, and unloving, and quick to criticize in an attempt to elevate themselves. What they didn't know was that Aunt Marie had virtually no money. She allowed me to oversee her finances, which was nothing more than fifteen thousand dollars divided equally between three Certificates of Deposit and a savings account with little more than eight thousand dollars in it. I had Marie agree to sign a limited Power of Attorney, which allowed me to take that fifteen thousand and invest it in the stock market. A much better place for it at the time.

After three years of caring for Aunt Marie, Leslie and I rushed down to Vineland to begin enacting our promise to her. Hospitalized by a stroke, Marie might no longer be able to live alone. In exchange for making me executor of her will and selling me her house for one dollar, she had made me promise I would never put her in a nursing home. She wanted to finish her life in her own home. When we arrived, Grace and Vincent were standing in the pale green hallway near the hospital room. Grace immediately sneered, "What are *you* going to do, Gary?"

"Yes, the doctor said her condition is something of a grey area," Vincent spouted as though he possessed complete knowledge and command of the crisis.

Her stroke was categorized as moderate-to-severe. The prognosis was that she would walk again, but when we arrived she was speaking gibberish. She recognized me immediately but there was enormous fear in her eyes. "Geckie," she whispered, attempting to speak my name. The stroke had left her with classic aphasia, both receptive and expressive. She needed rehab.

After several weeks of treatment at the Bacharach Center for Rehabilitation, I brought her home. Clutching the railing, concentrating hard, she climbed the three small steps to her back door. Once inside, she sat down in her usual chair at the kitchen table, trying to make it seem like life would simply go on as it had before. I put some coffee on and we sat quietly for a bit. Then she began talking to me. I couldn't make out what she was trying to say. Standing up, her voice grew louder as though maybe I couldn't hear her. "Rarrie ar ignasty yup?" she said, getting louder. Filling the kitchen with her rant, she started repeating herself, asking me the same question over and over, but I just couldn't figure it out. I could see that she was becoming irritated so I stood up, trying to calm her down, when she said something that sounded very harsh, almost like, "How could you be so stupid?" I remembered some pamphlets that Bacharach rehab had given me. "Here Aunt Marie, look," I said, calmly placing one on the kitchen table for her to see. It simply read "YOU HAD A STROKE." Looking at the pamphlet, she grabbed the table, collapsed in the chair, and put her head in her hands and began to cry. I hugged her tightly saying that everything would be all right.

Leslie and I had cleaned the house from stem to stern, which was badly needed. It was beginning to have that "old person" smell, and the once very nice, wall-to-wall green wool carpet in the living room had become black in the area where she had parked herself. I had already begun the process of getting her home health care along with whatever services the state and county could offer. I also hunted around for a private caregiver who could come in and prepare meals for her. I got a call back from my old friend Ed Dondero, still living nearby. His mother knew a woman from her senior dance club. Gloria T. would be available to help. I spent that entire week with Marie.

She had long ago stopped sleeping in her bedroom and had taken to reclining on the couch, letting the TV put her to sleep at night. As I got her set up in the living room, I noticed that she had the *TV Guide* at her side. This was a glimmer of hope; she had definitely been able to read the cover of that pamphlet and she seemed to be thumbing through the guide looking for her favorite shows. She loved *Matlock*, and I think she had a crush on Andy Griffith.

I thought it might be good for her to have some company, so against my better judgment I invited Grace and Vincent to come by and see her. They walked into the kitchen and said "Hello," Grace shooting bullets from her eyes. I suggested that they join Aunt Marie in the living room. I stayed with them for a moment and then returned to the kitchen and whatever song I was working on. I could hear Aunt Marie trying to talk to them for a few moments when they both burst out laughing. They actually thought that her inability to speak properly was funny. I was furious. After they left she walked into the kitchen, grabbed the pad and pen next to the phone, slammed the pad on the table, and proceeded to do a rather complicated triple-digit multiplication problem. When she finished she threw the pen down saying something that was meant to sound like, "There!" I stood up and gave her a big hug and a kiss and said, "Don't worry, Aunt Marie, I know you're not crazy." She had faith in me and needed for me to return that faith. She was my family and I needed to be there for her.

CHAPTER 18

SWEET MARIE

It was late November 1989 when I heard that a compilation of Pat Benatar's greatest hits was coming out. Released two years earlier in Europe, *Best Shots* was now going to be available in the States. It included all her hits: "Love Is a Battlefield," "We Belong," and of course, "Shadows of the Night."

This was very good news not only for me but for Aunt Marie as well. I had already begun funneling money to her as her savings account was tapped. I was trying to keep her 15K intact and growing. Gloria T. came three times a week to clean up, do laundry, and prepare meals Marie could simply put in the oven. Just before Marie's stroke, Grace and Vincent had bought Marie a microwave which she was scared to death to use. Months after giving her the appliance they stopped by and brought up their fabulous gift, apparently wanting to be thanked again.

As Marie was thanking them again for the despised appliance she used her undeniably jumbled speech, albeit dry humor, in stating the obvious, "If it weren't for you, I wouldn't have a microwave." Or at least that was what I could make out.

So finally I had set up everything that pertained to her daily care. I had arranged with Gloria T. to leave her pay on top of the refrigerator in a small bank envelope and had also hired a speech therapist to come by once a week. It finally seemed that everything would be running smoothly, so I felt secure enough to head back to the city for the week.

Midweek I got a call from Betty my adoption caseworker, saying she thought she might have some promising clues that she would follow up on. Because of her strict guidelines she wasn't able to share those leads with me. Naturally, I was excited, but I had so many balls in the air at the time that I really didn't think too much about the possibilities.

I had also begun putting some songs together to record as well as putting a new band together to play the club circuit downtown. I didn't have management at the time. Not being the greatest at self promotion it was hard to get people to show up for gigs. My "band" effort was short lived, so I just kept on writing. Although, at that time, I would say that my songs were more craft than inspiration. I just had too much on my plate.

When Leslie and I returned to Marie's, the following weekend everything seemed to be just fine until I got a phone call from Gloria T., the hired caregiver, saying that I had shorted her twenty dollars. I was mystified by this so I took special care that the next envelope I left would be absolutely correct. The next week she called again with the same complaint. I surmised that someone was stealing money from the envelope. Leslie and I arrived back at Marie's the following Friday night. I had a peculiar suspicion about this, so when we went to bed I purposely left my wallet on the kitchen table. When we woke up on Saturday morning my wallet lay open with the bills fanning out. I never left my wallet like that. It was always closed. I did a quick cash count and indeed a twenty was missing. There was only one conclusion. Rosa, the old Russian woman upstairs, had snuck onto the first floor from inside the house and was helping herself to money. Naturally when I confronted her she cried, "I no steal! I no steal!" She had actually been bilking my aunt for years by paying only two hundred dollars a month in rent. I told her that since she had no lease I would be doubling the rent. She called her daughter, who lived nearby but wanted little to do with her, with the intention that she might reason with me. I told her daughter, a woman in her mid-thirties, that her mother really needed help. "What kind of help?" she asked naively. "Professional," I snapped. Rosa would walk through the entire neighborhood every day picking up loose change and the odd bottle cap, only to pull you aside and say in a heavy Russian accent, "Look what I find!" She really needed professional supervision, so if she or her clueless daughter were unable or unwilling to pay the four hundred a month, still very reasonable for the entire second floor, then I would have to ask her to leave.

I hated being a hardnose, but this woman had taken advantage of my aunt for far too long, even if she wasn't right in the head, which she wasn't. Marie knew that her rent was ridiculously low but she didn't have the heart to ever raise it. So Rosa's daughter helped her pack and she left, which of course ended the mysteriously vanishing twenty dollar bill routine. I was fully aware that having someone in the house in case something should happen was a good thing, but I just couldn't abide a liar and a thief. Besides, Rosa could barely take care of herself let alone anyone else. I had already gotten Marie a "life alert" system with the "panic button" that she would wear around her neck should anything go wrong. That along with all the home health care people coming in and out left me feeling fairly comfortable.

In the coming months, Aunt Marie showed a marked improvement. We were actually beginning to figure out her peculiar lingo especially when it was linked with her body language. She was even able to present us with something of a grocery list when we arrived for the weekend. Naturally there were misspelled words with just a touch of confusion. "Yam" meant ham and "tucky" meant turkey but she was really trying her best to return to some degree of normalcy.

One Saturday morning Leslie had made us breakfast of bacon and eggs. It was a sunny, crisp winter day. Leslie and I had errands to do later that afternoon so the three of us sat down to eat. Marie seemed to stare off into space for a bit then suddenly she slammed down her empty coffee cup saying, "I just wish someone would come over and 'tie me up' once in a while." I spit my mouthful of coffee halfway across the table but instantly knew that what she meant was that she just wanted someone to come over and "TAKE HER OUT" once in a while. Her diction was certainly improving.

We would usually go to Leslie's parents in Pennsylvania for Thanksgiving and then drive down to see Marie. This particular year we thought that it might be nice to put together a proper Thanksgiving dinner for her so we pulled in with a twelve-pound turkey in the trunk. Saturday morning Leslie began to prepare the bird for the oven; we already had prepared the stuffing so it was just a matter of getting the bird into a proper pan, which unfortunately Marie didn't have. We had to use something that almost resembled a cookie sheet, which was a poor replacement for a deep baking pan. We got the bird into the oven and told Marie that we still had some shopping to do, so she was now in charge of the turkey. We ended up taking longer than expected and upon our return Marie was at the back door in a panic. We ran into the kitchen and we were immediately hit by thick smoke. Apparently the fat from the turkey couldn't be contained by the pan and was dripping to the bottom of the oven. We opened the kitchen windows and put the bird outside in the garbage. After we had cleaned up we told Aunt Marie that we would go out for dinner. We took her to the Buena Tavern, one of her favorite places to go when Uncle Tony was still around. To Aunt Marie all liquor was simply "scotch," but she would point to my drink, a vodka martini already on the table, and nod her head "yes." What she drank really didn't matter too much to her as long as she was out and about.

The year was 1996 and Aunt Marie was turning eighty-one, so we took her to dinner once again at the Buena Tavern, this time joined by my old friend Ed Dondero and his wife Dominie. We had arranged for a small Italian layer cake with a cream filling and covered in white icing to be brought to the table at the end of our meal. The number 81 in blue icing and a single candle topped the cake. She chuckled as we lit the candle and she drew an invisible "number 1" in the air, but as she did this her eyes began to drift from side to side and her shoulders slumped a bit. I feared that she might be having a ministroke and her drooping head was aimed squarely at the cake. I pulled my cell phone out, ready to call 911, but almost immediately we managed to sit her up straight and in a few seconds she snapped back.

We fell into the routine of traveling to see Marie every other weekend. Leslie and I began to stop at a local bar before showing up at Marie's house. We had to loosen up before we sat down to the forty-five minute rant that she would unload as soon as we walked in the door. She would go on and on about Gloria T. and how she always showed up when *Matlock* was on, annoying her to no end, and of course there were other indiscernible stories about her home health care worker or the speech therapist, as well as lengthy lists of things that she needed done. At times she seemed downright ungrateful but then I would remember how terribly frustrating all of this must be for her. We were so fortunate that she was still able to get around the house and even bathe herself without assistance, but all of this was still a big strain on us. The constant driving back and forth over a hundred miles each way, sleeping on the floor, our ankles being bitten by dust mites, was definitely taking its toll. We had already been married for several years and had begun to think about starting a family, but those plans had to be set aside. Aunt Marie came first, for now.

There were so many questions that I should have asked Aunt Marie before she had her stroke. Questions about my adoptive mother and why she was the way she was. Did something traumatic happen to her when she was a young girl? I had often wondered if she might have been molested or raped when she was young. She certainly had little interest in sex with my father but that could have been more about my father. So many questions. Marie was full of secrets that I would now never know. Whatever those questions were, I had been too timid to inquire. Now given her aphasia any probing into the past would be impossible. What I did know was that they had once lived in Brooklyn and their father, Peter, was a hat blocker on Delancey Street in lower Manhattan. He would walk over the Williamsburg Bridge every day to get to his job. He made bathtub gin during prohibition and would trade his gin with his boss for a week's vacation for his family in Saugerties, New York, his employer's summer home. My mother and Marie were half sisters and that was never explained, in fact it was something of a family secret. I knew that Peter's first wife had passed away but he didn't remarry until years later. One day he just picked up and moved his family from Brooklyn to a small farm in Vineland. Back then Vineland had something of a Ukrainian enclave that was attracting many others to move to the area. So my mother, Marie, and their brother John spent their late childhood living on the farm. In those days farmhands were basically drifters who would stay and work for a while, being provided with room and board, and then would eventually move on. Had one of these transients ruined my mother's life in some way, or was she emotionally wounded by something else? These were questions that would never be addressed. Those answers would have shed light on just about everything, but now I was left to guess what might have been the truth. Whatever it was, the lasting impact on my mother had been passed on to me. The shadows of a dysfunctional and traumatic childhood continued to shadow my life.

Aunt Marie was now getting better and better. Although communicating with her was still a challenge, her speech was improving, her attitude was generally upbeat, and what memories she had of my uncle's suicide seemed to be buried down deep.

We were approaching six years of looking after her when one day I got a phone call saying that Aunt Marie was in the hospital again. She had suffered congestive heart failure. I hopped in the car and drove down there as fast as I could.

She would remain hospitalized for more than a week. I stayed at her house and visited daily. This is where I was really needed because I was fairly reliable at decoding what she was trying to say and that was a very big help to her doctors.

When Grace and Vincent would visit it was plain to see that she was becoming increasingly disenchanted with them. She was finally seeing them as the opportunists they really were.

They were only interested in the money that she didn't have and the house that had already been sold to me, although they didn't know that at the time. I never said a bad word about Grace and Vincent in front of Marie; she was sensing something about them all on her own.

They lived about a mile or so from Marie's house but were perfectly happy to watch me jump through hoops of fire in order to keep my aunt's life together. They never offered to help in any way. It was painfully obvious that they were just waiting for her to die so that the will would be executed. Just before Marie was to be released the doctor suggested to me that she go back into rehab. Bacharach Rehabilitation was not known to accept repeaters. It was a struggle but somehow I convinced their administration to admit Marie for a second time, something that was nearly unprecedented. Since she was bedridden for nearly two weeks she would need help to become ambulatory again. I remember the last few days of her stay there, the nurses were putting her through the last phases of her therapy. Leslie and I were with her as they gave her a "final exam" which involved her walking around a gym and displaying with confidence that she could adequately move on her own. There were several other patients in the gym all there for the same reason. I leaned over and whispered in Marie's ear, "You're gonna have to do some somersaults if you want to go home." She seemed to understand exactly what I was saying. When it came her turn she shot up and with all the physical grace of a swan began to move around the room like she was doing some kind of Olympic gymnastic routine. Everyone just watched in amazement, especially me.

When she was done she came back to her folding chair and glanced up at me as if to say, "How's that?!" Leslie and I started laughing and we both gave her a big kiss saying to her, "You're out!"

CHAPTER 19

THE PEAR TREE

Back in New York I got another call from Betty my caseworker. There had been a few leads, but once again she could not share any details. All I would learn was that they were dead ends but she had discovered a new clue, and based on what investigation she had done so far, she thought this time she was finally on the right trail. Even more hopeful, she said she'd spoken with the woman she suspected was actually my birthmother, but the woman on the phone was distraught and not making much sense. Betty asked her to take down her phone number and call her back when she felt better. That call never came.

So maybe that was it, that would be as close as I would ever come to finding her. A feeling in my gut was telling me that Betty had indeed spoken with my birthmother, but what if she wanted nothing to do with me? I hadn't come all this way to face rejection but I certainly couldn't force the issue either. My heart sank to the pit of my stomach. My childhood flashed through my brain. Those early fantasies of having my real parents return to rescue me had been thwarted. My delusions of being whisked away into an imaginary life of opulence by the people who had temporarily forgotten about me were dashed. I was once again darkly adrift at sea.

The following two weekends, I began to notice that Aunt Marie seemed distant. She appeared to be getting shaky, losing her grip. She appeared frail and experienced moments of confusion. I suspected that she might be slipping into depression. We had gotten her a hospital bed so she stopped sleeping on the couch. She hadn't slept in a bed since Uncle Tony had committed suicide. Hopefully she would find some comfort there. It seemed like she was growing weary of the fight and might be succumbing to the inevitable.

She called me into her bedroom on Sunday morning and showed me a tissue that she had just coughed into. Its color was a dark green and I knew immediately this was very serious. I packed up some of her things and Leslie and I drove her to Kessler Hospital in Hammonton not too far from Vineland. I went through the admission process with her. We stayed with her there as long as we could. I forced myself into believing that she was in good hands. Sadly, we returned to the house to pack our things, preparing to leave. Just as we were ready to walk out the door the phone rang, and it was the hospital calling to tell me to pick her up. I was already very concerned that she had pneumonia. I inquired about her x-rays. They told me that everything appeared to be normal and to come get her. How could this be? She had almost every symptom of either acute bronchitis or worse given the dark phlegm that she showed me. She should have been put on antibiotics immediately. I was angry but we got into the car and went to get her. When Leslie and I arrived, we learned that the hospital had given her no medication at all but instead planned to simply release her.

Once home, we got her settled in. This time I put her on the couch so she could watch TV and hopefully fall asleep. Together we made sure that everything was in place. Unfortunately, we had to leave her there and head back to New York. I was praying that she would be all right.

Almost as soon as we got back to New York the phone rang. Marie had used her life alert to call an ambulance and someone from Kessler Hospital was calling to inform us that she had been readmitted.

At around three in the morning we got another call from the hospital telling us that she was in Intensive Care and was being administered a "cocktail" of antibiotics. She indeed had pneumonia and I was really pissed.

We decided to stay in New York and wait 'til morning. When early morning came we got another call from the hospital and this time the voice on the other end simply said, "I'm so sorry . . . she's gone." I think I may have dropped the phone. I simply fell apart.

Leslie drove as I was in pieces. The hospital was on the way to Marie's house so we stopped there first to collect her things and take care of any paperwork that needed to be addressed. I signed a small pile of forms and was given the jewelry she had been wearing . . . a gold band and chain and an amethyst ring that she was so fond of.

I cashed out Marie's stocks to pay for the funeral. We decided to combine her service with a Mass in her honor, all to take place at St. Michael's in Minotola. The details of this become hazy for me. I was not really all there and Leslie took over in taking care of the details. She was my rock. I don't know that I ever could have taken care of Marie on my own.

What I remember of the funeral is that her coffin was open and situated at the front of the church just below the altar. For some reason I was able to handle an open casket this time. Maybe I had matured. She was to be buried with her favorite amethyst ring on her finger, a ring that Grace had been eyeing for years. Grace and Vincent sat on the right side of the church with their family taking up the front pews. This place was usually reserved for the family members who had paid for the funeral and naturally they knew that, but they sat there out of defiance just the same. They seemed as cold and distant as usual, or maybe they were just chomping at the bit to get to that will. After the burial some people stopped by the house to pay their respects. Even my not-so-beloved "Holy Roller" Aunt Helen showed up with my cousin Edith. We had gotten some deli food, chicken salad, potato salad, and we had the coffee going. Some people stayed for a bit to share their stories about Marie but when Vincent and Grace came by they only stayed for five minutes and they were gone. It was over.

In the coming months we would come down to the empty house and spend the weekend just to get out of the city. We decided to renovate the second floor in the hopes of getting a tenant. Since we had just inherited a house, we decided to put our signature on it, make it our own. During one of these renovation weekends Grace and Vincent called saying that they would like to come over. We all sat at the kitchen table and they began to interrogate me. "When are you going to execute the will?" they demanded. I told them that Marie's money was gone so there was no point in dealing with the will. They sat, arms folded and squirming around in their seats, like five year olds who had just been bullied out of their lunch money. They appeared ridiculous, as though they were about to accuse me of stealing Aunt Marie's vast fortune. If I hadn't been so angry I would have been rolling around on the floor laughing.

Then Grace said, "I would like something to remember her by, I want to see her jewelry," in a demanding tone. Leslie went into Marie's bedroom and brought out a small wooden box, then sat down at the kitchen table opening the box. Leslie then offered her a few gold chains, which she immediately grabbed trying to catch a glimpse of what was inside the box. What she really wanted was the ring that Marie was buried with. I knew a bit about precious stones and that amethyst was in fact artificial. Then Grace went on about Marie's cut crystal. I found a suitable cardboard box and we placed Marie's bowls and such in the box and the two of them left without saying anything. About two hours later as we were going through the garage trying to assess what needed to go, Grace pulled into the driveway and put the cardboard box of Marie's bowls on the ground, got back into her car, and sped off. Upon closer inspection Leslie told me that the bowls were cut glass and not crystal. I suppose Grace had figured that out as well. That really stuck in my throat, but the good news was that we probably wouldn't be seeing either of them again.

Leslie and I continued to empty out the garage and the first floor, placing unwanted items on the curb. When we woke up in the morning and looked outside mostly all of it was gone. The little hamlet of Minotola where Marie had lived was situated just outside of Vineland. When I was a kid it was a very nice place to be. All the houses were beautifully kept and it was quiet and peaceful, but Minotola had since fallen on hard times. The local three man police department was now busier than ever.

We finally rented the upstairs to a young couple. They were young hippie types. He had long hair and she had a huge tattoo on her back but otherwise seemed all right. It turned out that the husband/boyfriend had a habit of getting into bar fights. We eventually found out that he was also involved in the local drug trade and was now on the run.

One night as Leslie was sleeping, I put some water on to boil for pasta and then sat in the living room watching TV wearing only a tee shirt. Suddenly I began seeing lights moving around the dining room. The local police walked in the back door looking for the guy upstairs. They came into the living room and asked who I was. I told them that I owned the house and that it had once belonged to my aunt. Starting for the bedroom, I asked them to stop because my wife was sleeping.

They looked down and then I looked down and realized that I wasn't wearing any pants. I asked them to wait and I quickly grabbed some shorts to put on. They inquired about the guy upstairs and I told them that I hadn't seen him in a while. Finally, they wanted to get to the second floor; I just pointed to the door off the dining room and they were gone. I knew that I shouldn't have allowed them to go up there. They didn't have a search warrant but I was so shaken that I just wasn't thinking straight. They let themselves out through the second floor exit and didn't come back to bother with me. Maybe this "landlord" thing was going to be more dicey than I thought.

Several months and a couple of tenants went by until we found someone reliable. With that we decided to rent out the first floor as well. I knew that I should have just sold the house but it had so much sentimental value to me, having spent so much time there as a kid. I couldn't bring myself to part with it or the old pear tree. So through a friend I found someone who was willing to manage the property.

Leslie and I began looking for something else to buy. We wanted a place on the Jersey Shore. We considered Cape May but it was just too far of a drive from the city. We looked in other towns, but prices were high. So finally we checked out Ocean City, a barrier island just below Atlantic City. I used to go there when I was a kid, and Leslie's aunt had owned a house there. Only two and a half hours from New York, it seemed like the right fit. Originally founded by Mennonites, Ocean City was a "dry town" so you wouldn't have the college keg parties going on all around you. It was just a nice quiet "wonder bread" kind of place with beautiful beaches. We finally settled on a house that was in need of work but had great bones. It was built in 1927 so it had some old-world charm. Along with three stories it included a two bedroom apartment over the garage in back. This was a lot of house and now we would be up to our eyeballs in the "landlord" thing. We did a lot of Dumpster diving for old doors, glass doorknobs, crown molding, anything that could be reused for restoration. I began to go down there for a week at a time just to work on the place and do some writing. Off-season, it could be a wonderful place to escape to.

I remembered that Betty my caseworker had mentioned that she was relocating to a new office in Vineland, my hometown, a little more than thirty minutes away. So I thought that since she was now so close by I could give her a call and possibly take her out for lunch to put a face on things. So with some hesitation I called her office. " Oh dear, she just broke her ankle and will be out for about eight weeks. You should call back then," I was told. "How awful," I thought. She had told me how much she loved to play golf.

CHAPTER 20

BONNIE JEANNE

I t was a Monday in the spring of '98 and I was sleeping in. I had been up all night working on a song, and Leslie was already at work when the phone rang. I rolled out of bed; it was Betty calling me. We had not spoken for over eight weeks, and I had just left a message for her the day before. Asking how she was, she barked, "Fine! Now grab a pen and paper," tersely adding, "If anything more serious had happened to me, no one would have picked up your file ever again." I was still not fully awake but she got me scrambling. She made me promise emphatically not to tell anyone about the information that she was about to give me. Betty had once expressed her affinity for thinking outside the box, and just how much she really loved her job. I sensed that she was about to blatantly circumvent its guidelines without prior consent from my birthmother. She was breaking all the rules. She was about to tell me exactly what she knew for sure.

Betty began with my mother's name, "Jeanne." "Your mother was born on February 6, 1932," she said. "You also have a sister named Dianne Ingemi who is an attorney working in

Cherry Hill, New Jersey." Then she gave me her office number. I wrote furiously, hoping that I was getting it all down. She said a few more words and then made me promise again that I would never breathe a word of this to anyone. I promised, and she hung up. I had trouble setting the phone in its cradle because my hands were shaking. I called Leslie, who came home for an hour or so to be with me.

I had only one phone number to call but this would be the most difficult phone call that I had ever made. I didn't feel comfortable making a cold call, so in thinking it through, I devised a ruse to get past the receptionist. So with Leslie at my side I dialed the number of the law firm. When the call was picked up I asked to speak to Dianne Ingemi. "Can I tell her who's calling?" asked a voice.

"I have some information about a case she's working on and thought she'd find it useful, but I'd prefer to remain anonymous," I said nervously. She put me right through.

"Hello, this is Dianne," said another voice.

I guardedly said, "Hello, my name is David Byron." Then cautiously I began with questions. "Is your mother's name Jeanne?" I started.

"Yes," she answered quickly.

Pausing, I then asked, "Was she . . . was she born on February 6th, 1932?"

Dianne then stopped me, asking, "Who is this?"

After a brief but seemingly endless silence, clearing my throat I answered by saying, "I have every reason to believe that I am your brother." Then came a very pregnant pause. "Oh no . . . " I thought. Would she say that she didn't believe me and just hang up the phone? Or even worse, say that she already knew about me and wasn't interested? I didn't hear a click.

"Go on," she said. I carefully explained that I thought I was born in Trenton or possibly Freehold but wasn't sure, and that I was raised in Vineland, and then began to nervously rattle off a bunch of other things that I don't even recall. I was so excited I just started to babble. She was actually very receptive, almost empathetic, and even mentioned that she had always felt her mother's secretiveness about something. But she could never even imagine what it was. She actually gave me her home number saying that I could call her later that evening. I thanked her several times. Even as I was hanging up the phone I could feel myself shudder inside. This moment felt like a glimpse a performer has from backstage through the slit in the curtain, the audience sitting out there, waiting, before the show begins.

Leslie had to return to work. Suddenly anxiety closed in and I was overwhelmed. Once again, like in childhood, I couldn't breathe. I sat down on the bed and began to cry. I was as elated as I was petrified.

I called Dianne that night and we spoke for almost an hour. "So what do you do for a living?" she asked.

"I'm a musician, but mostly a songwriter," I told her.

"Wow, my husband is a musician, I mean he's an attorney, but he plays guitar and bass," she gushed. "You know, I have six sisters," she said.

"Oh my . . . six, really?" I gasped, not knowing how to respond.

During our conversation on Tuesday night she began by saying, "Oh I forgot to mention, the bunch of us are from two different fathers, and I actually have a fraternal twin." Not only was this interesting but I was so happy and relieved by how open she was with me. We agreed to speak again the following night. On Wednesday evening she said pensively,

"I'm planning to bring Mom dinner tomorrow night. I think that maybe I'll bring along some old family scrapbooks for us to look at together." She seemed to be thinking out loud. It struck me that Dianne had it in her mind that she might gently broach this dramatic new event with her mother by using her scrapbooks as a means to an end.

The following night after dinner she and her mother sat down and began to go through Dianne's family photos. Her mother brought out a bunch of old photos as well. While they were looking, Dianne noticed one of her young mother standing in front of a building with a large group of girls all around the same age. There were nuns standing on either side of the group. "Mom, is this you here in this group shot? Where is this?" asked Dianne. "Oh my mother had to send me there once when she felt that she couldn't take care of me," she said, getting up to go to the bathroom. When her mother left the room, Dianne slipped the picture out of the sleeve to look at the back of the photo and found printed there the words "Freehold, New Jersey." When she returned, Dianne calmly said, "Mom, there's a man who's been calling me. He's claiming to be my brother . . . " Her mother sank back in her green comfy chair, became teary-eyed, then looked up at Dianne and in a quivering voice said, "Honey . . . he probably is."

Months earlier my caseworker, Betty, had sent me some letters written by my birthmother to her own caseworker. They were handwritten and physically edited, which is to say that portions of the letters were literally cut away with scissors. Even though some of them were two pages in length and written on such nice "flowery" dime-store stationery, they didn't reveal very much. The guts were gone. I dug them up and faxed them to Dianne's office. Dianne seemed to recognize her mother's handwriting. I later found out this indeed was the woman who Betty, my caseworker, had spoken with. She sounded distraught over the phone because Betty had called her only a day or so after her beloved second husband had died of a sudden heart attack. No wonder the call was not returned. When I spoke to Dianne the following day she told me what had happened. Certainly I was happy that at last I had found her, but I began to realize the trauma that my birthmother must have dealt with all these years. Such a deep dark secret to keep hidden away for such a very long time. As I reflected on my own traumatic childhood, I tried to imagine what she had suffered. I supposed that in any adoption, trauma is a two-way street. Finally I asked Dianne, "What if you and your husband brought your mother to Ocean City for the day so we could all finally meet?"

Dianne said she thought it prudent to call her mother's doctor to see if she could withstand such a meeting, as she suffered from a heart condition. The doctor suggested a Nitroglycerin pill thirty minutes before she would see me. But when Dianne and her husband, Scott, got to her mother's to pick her up, she had decided against it. She covered her face with her hands crying, "I'm not worthy! . . . I'm not worthy!" Thankfully, after calming her down Dianne was able to change her mind. Dianne called to tell me what happened but assured me that they were on their way. Her husband, Scott, also an attorney, thought that this whole thing reeked of something underhanded. "He's after our money, I just know it," I would later be told he repeated as he drove. "I smell something rotten", he said.

They arrived late Saturday morning. It was a sunny day in Ocean City. Winter was at an end, and I could hear the waves from the window I had cracked in the bathroom. I was just getting out of the shower, so I quickly got dressed. Leslie ushered them in and sat them down in the living room. We still had all the threadbare furniture that had come with the house, but it was a warm and comfortable room just the same. I walked in still buttoning my shirt with a head of wet hair. Scott's jaw dropped as he sat up in the rocking chair and took a good look at me. He was realizing that I looked just like my mom. I spontaneously went over to my nervous fair-skinned mother, put my arm around her, and kissed her cheek. Touching her fine, reddish-blonde hair, I sat beside her. I so wanted to put her mind at rest and relieve her from this heavy burden that she had carried all this time. So gently I whispered in her ear, "I just want you to know . . . I'm not angry." She seemed greatly relieved and we just sat there and hugged each other, really hard. Then handing her one of the notes she had written I asked, "Is this your handwriting?" She took it in her trembling hand and began reading it saying, "Yes . . . Yes it is."

Leslie prepared some chicken salad for lunch, I played the board game "Othello" with Scott, and he beat me. Then we all walked to the beach and eventually went out for dinner because no one wanted the day to end. During dinner my mother said, "You know I always believed that this would happen one day. I'm psychic and I'm sure that you are too."

"Funny, I've always believed that about myself, and I also always believed we would meet, and I'm so grateful," I said, touching her hand. I didn't have any recent pictures of myself to give to her but I had just finished a new record and there was a full length picture of me in a "mod" suit on the cover. I had a bunch of copies and gave them to my mother in case she should decide to tell my other sisters about me. We finally hugged and kissed good night and I said that I hoped to hear from them soon. That night I slept like a baby . . . a baby who had just finally found his mother.

The next morning my newly found mother called a family meeting at Dianne's house. She didn't tell anyone what it was about but insisted that all sisters be present. When they arrived in Cherry Hill she sat them down at the dining room table and began to place my CD in front of each one. Donna the eldest quizzically asked why she was getting a CD when she didn't own a disk player. One of the grandkids walked by the table, saw the album cover and declared, "Hey, that guy looks just like Grandma!" And that's when they were all finally told my mother's lifelong secret. Dianne called saying, "Well, they all want to meet you. Do you feel like driving to Cherry Hill?"

"I'll be there in an hour!" I chuckled.

Leslie had to drive, I was just way too nervous. The fifty-minute drive to Cherry Hill seemed like forever. My mind was on overdrive. As we pulled up to Dianne's suburban, white split-level house, I saw a woman standing in the street sobbing. It was my eldest sister, Donna. Then the front door of the house opened and one by one all my sisters came running out yelling gleefully and surrounding Leslie and me on the front lawn. I felt both tension and loving acceptance at the same time. The moment was as awkward as it was completely natural. I introduced Leslie to them and one by one they introduced themselves with a hug and a kiss. I was still very nervous and some of them seemed unsure of themselves as well, but just the same we all laughed and cried together. We huddled there together talking for a moment, getting in a second hug. The rest of my new family was waiting in the house so eventually we all went inside.

They had many questions and so did I. My mother explained that she hid the pregnancy from her own mother for fear that she, being only twenty at the time, would have been forced into a "back alley" abortion. By the time that her mother found out it was already too late. She also hid my birth from her first husband. Jeanne's third marital birth was with my fraternal twin sisters, Denise and Dianne. Her first husband, who desperately wanted a boy, got so mad that he hung up the phone on the doctor who was delivering the good news. He didn't speak to my mother for two weeks. They eventually divorced.

Someone pointed out that my moniker was D. L. Byron. Three of my sisters were D. L.'s. Donna Lee, Denise Louise, and Dianne Lynne. My other sisters' names were Toni, Sandy, Kimberly, and Jeannie. I had picked my professional name David Leigh Byron out of a hat, so to speak. It was a crazy psychic connection that I had picked D.L. My mother told me that she also had given birth to a stillborn son whose name would have been Michael. To add to the growing coincidences, I had picked the name Michael as my confirmation name so many years before. She went on to say that she too was born out of wedlock and that as a child she would often visit the man who sired her. She told me that he owned The Music Inn, the big music store on Landis Avenue in Vineland. So in other words, I may have actually bought my first guitar from my biological grandfather! Which meant that at any time while in school, I might have been sitting across from a blood cousin. It was all getting a bit confusing and on some level, the details didn't even matter. By that point I had already decided not to climb up my grandfather's family tree. What had just happened was enough for me. Still I was curious about my father. My mother couldn't remember his name, just that he was Northern Italian and had offered her a ride home on a rainy evening. We stayed for hours laughing, playing with their kids and trading stories. I felt a real connection with them and yet there was a silent distance. I hadn't grown up with them so we didn't share a history, we had only blood in common. I wanted to get to know them all especially my mother of course. Eventually it came time to go, so Leslie and I said a tearful goodbye and headed back to New York. On the drive home Leslie and I couldn't stop talking about what had happened. She was so supportive. I know I couldn't have done it without her. That was quite a day. I was overjoyed, shocked, and confused all at the same time. So many questions were answered but I still had so many more. The past forty eight hours were so much more than I could have ever imagined. It's such a difficult thing to explain in words because there really is nothing to compare it to. That day was the culmination of years of yearning, decades of hope and heartbreak all coming together in one stunning life-changing event. I had heard of people finding each other after years of separation but nothing like this. This was like winning the lottery.

I'm sure that Scott was relieved to find that I actually had my own money, and everyone was impressed that I had written "Shadows of the Night." But all of that became nothing more than fluff and fodder. I was just hopeful that our new relationship would stand the test of time. As I said, we had only blood in common. No history. So it was difficult to speculate as to how all this would play out going forward.

Over the following years we went down for every holiday, often doing double duty between my new family and Leslie's in Pennsylvania. It was great for me to be around so many people that I actually had a connection with. I had already come to grips with my delusions of being spirited away by my fictional "real" parents. I did, however, feel something real here with all these new people. Something that I had never felt as a child. I discovered early on that there was something of a silent inequity among my sisters. A few of them had done well in life while some others hadn't done quite as well. Kimberly, or Kee as everyone called her, seemed to have struggled with money the most yet she seemed to be quite content. The one sister who didn't seem so particularly happy was Donna. It seemed to me like she was holding on to anger or unhappiness as though it validated her somehow. I sensed in her a deep displeasure that she would not easily forgive. She and another sister, Jeannie, lived in Vineland. I could have stumbled right over either of them at the Shop Rite when we were taking care of Aunt Marie. All of my sisters lived in South Jersey. It was odd to think that we had been so close in proximity all along.

A few months after the glorious reunion, I invited everyone to a solo acoustic performance that I was doing at the new Gaslight on 14th Street. Mostly everyone made the trip although Mom didn't feel well enough to come. I was already a "regular" at the club. The Gaslight did a pretty good bar business being located in a trendy part of town. There was a sizable crowd that night. As I looked out from the stage I could see my sisters and their families sprinkled through the dimly lit room. After the first song I paused to tell the audience an abbreviated version of the story and that my new family was here for me. The whole place went crazy. That night was very special. A couple of months later everyone came back to New York again to visit us at our loft on Grand Street, and Mom also came along that time. Most of them had really never spent any time in the city, so I think it was exciting for them. My psychic Mom mentioned to me that she saw a ghost in my apartment. I had always known of a presence there, although not malevolent like in the house on Roberts Boulevard as a child. When I first took the loft I walked into the kitchen one morning to see a woman on her knees with her back to me scrubbing the floor, and just like that she was gone. Another time I was in the kitchen and I heard opera music coming from the next room. It sounded like it was being played on an old Victrola but as soon as I went to investigate the music stopped. Sometimes when I played the piano I could smell a very fragrant perfume close by. That happened more than a few times even when others were present. Everyone could smell it. The loft had been a wedding gown manufacturer in the mid-to-late 1800's, and you could even tell just by looking at the interior layout of the space. What was our living room was likely the showroom and the back area was probably where the gowns were made. There was even a back corner office, which then served as my study. In that room I had placed all the occult books and manuscripts that I had collected over the years. I had even set up a personal altar as a designated place for meditation. It was a very unusual and charming space.

In August of 2000 Leslie told me that we were starting a family of our own. I was both elated and scared to death. When I was young I never imagined myself married let alone being a parent. Now it appeared that I was being given a golden opportunity. I would take on the responsibility of trying not to make the same mistakes that my parents had made. That would be a monumental assignment.

CHAPTER 21

DANICA

When I gave my new family the news everyone was happy for us, especially my mother who already had seven grandchildren. There were tons of congratulatory phone calls and loving emails. Everyone was excited. Dianne began pressing and questioning me about moving to Ocean City as the school system was fairly decent there. I guess she thought that when city dwellers started families they immediately left for the suburbs. I quickly told her that it simply wasn't our plan.

On the same day that Leslie found out she was pregnant she also learned that her father was seriously ill. Web had pancreatic cancer. This put a hard spin on things, but Leslie seemed to believe that her dad would recover. I knew how serious his situation was.

Carl Webster Haag, Leslie's dad, was a quiet man who once headed up a local bank and eventually left to become chief financial officer for a large auction company. This was an easy, almost "semi-retirement" job for him that allowed him and Joan to travel a bit and got them both out on the road. I think that he enjoyed that job very much, but after some persuasion from Leslie's mom, he decided to retire. That's when he fell ill, almost immediately.

Leslie was extremely pregnant, in her eighth month, and we were enjoying a quiet weekend down in Ocean City. We were out running errands on Saturday afternoon when Leslie's water broke. She had gone into the Rite Aid and when she returned to the car her jeans were soaked. I, not quite ready for the inevitable, had to ask, "Are you sure you're not just a little leaky?"

"No . . . I need to call the doctor immediately," she said nervously, "I'm not due for another month!" Our doctor told us to hit the highway and race back to New York. We headed north on the Garden State Parkway doing about ninety miles an hour, praying that a state trooper would pull us over and escort us, but no such luck. We got to NYU Medical in one piece, got signed in, and Leslie received an epidural. Staying in the delivery room for what seemed like hours, we patiently waited for Leslie to begin having contractions. She was quite comfortably in bed and I sat in a chair in the corner of the room staring at her, contemplating my fate and occasionally glancing at the shiny linoleum floor. At around two in the morning hunger got the best of me so I ordered in some Chinese food. Naturally, as soon as the food arrived Leslie began to give birth. The entire delivery room became electrified. Our doctor was great but the nurses were fantastic. They kept yelling for Leslie to push. At one point, Leslie said, "I'm afraid that I'm going to push something out of my butt!" To which one of the nurses replied, "Don't worry, I will clean you!" Within moments the doctor was holding something that resembled a dripping wet eggplant. This was our girl. On April 8, 2001, just after three in the morning Leslie delivered our first. Dr. Frank, our OBGYN, turned to me asking,

"Would you like to cut the cord?" offering me surgical scissors. I was a little shaky but I did it. Even though at that moment our daughter might have looked a bit like a wrinkled-up garden vegetable, she was gorgeous. "So beautiful," I thought as I placed that little nugget into Leslie's waiting arms. It was then decided that Leslie would stay overnight so I headed home to grab a couple hours of sleep. By mid-morning I arrived back at the hospital to find that my sister-in-law Patti had driven Leslie's parents up to the hospital to see the baby. Leslie's dad was jaundiced and had to sit in a wheelchair; it seemed the end was near.

We had already converted my study into a nursery, so we proudly brought the baby home to Grand Street. We had done quite a bit of work on the place. I had exposed a brick wall in the kitchen, we had a nice dining area, and an adjacent space that was now set up as our bedroom. The small room in the back corner of the loft which used to be my study, now the nursery, it was freshly painted and appropriately decorated. A brand-new wooden crib was already in place. We had tucked a yellow duckie comforter inside and had hung a "moon & stars" mobile above. We were ready to receive our little girl.

We were both scared senseless and what about a name? I wanted to keep the "D. L." tradition going so I began the name search. Danielle came to mind but I dismissed that as being too commonplace, and finally I came across the name Danica (in Eastern European: Danishka) which meant "morning star." It seemed like a rather fitting name since she was born so early in the morning, but what to do about the middle name? Leslie's grandmother's middle name was Lenore so there we had our D. L., Danica Lenore Byron.

She was so tiny and so beautiful. She didn't come with a manual, and I was clueless. But soon I was an expert at changing diapers. So fragile, we bathed her in the kitchen sink after which we would lay her on a towel which was waiting on the counter to wrap her up like a little burrito.

Everything was initially going just fine with one exception. I had a very jealous bird on my hands. Ming, my Blue Front Amazon, was extremely threatened and immediately made that perfectly clear. Parrots are possessive pets, so when we brought the baby home, the bird went completely nuts and literally began to scream day and night. Danica soon developed colic and was crying all the time; no one was getting any sleep. "That's it!" I finally shouted, "we're packing up everyone and going down to Ocean City for maternity leave!" We strapped the birdcage on top of the SUV and headed for South Jersey.

I was hoping that my "parrot" problem would now come to an end, and it did . . . just not the end that I anticipated. When we got there I put Ming's cage on the front porch. It was just warm enough for her to be outside, plus I put some heavy blankets over her cage for warmth but left it open in front so she could see outside. This didn't stop the bird from screaming, so after a day or two, I moved her cage into the garage. I would go out there in the morning to give her food and water when eventually it hit me that what I was doing was borderline inhumane. I couldn't keep her in the garage forever. So sadly, I looked for a pet store that might take her. I found a shop right in town so again I put her big cage on the roof of the car and placed Ming into a small carry cage on the seat next to me. I had to cover it because I was too sad to look at her for very long; after all, by then we had been together for seventeen years.

The shop agreed to take both the bird and the cage and promised to find her a good home. Once Ming was settled in around other birds she became perfectly calm. After all those years of being with her, I said my goodbyes and went back to the house.

A couple of days later we got a call from Leslie's mom saying that her father was in the hospital and probably didn't have much time left. I was nursing what felt like a mild case of bronchitis and I didn't even want to be around the baby let alone Leslie's dad, so I thought it best to stay behind. Leslie and the baby went to suburban Philadelphia to see her father for the last time. When she returned she told me that after arriving she put Danica in her father's lap as he sat up in bed. A smile came to his face, then after a few moments he seemed to speak to someone, something that sounded like, "I'm not ready yet," and a few moments later he simply passed away. I felt terrible that I wasn't with her. I did everything that I could to console her as we prepared for the funeral. A few days later at a local church in Lansdale the service was held. Hundreds of people had come to pay their respects. As a banker, her father had given small business loans to a number of very grateful people who were then able to put their lives in order. They shared their stories and condolences in a grieving line that seemed to go on for days. The minister was in the middle of a solemn and particularly touching eulogy when Danica suddenly exploded with diarrhea. I mean that quite literally, it was as though a bomb had gone off. We had to move her to the sacristy to get her and ourselves cleaned up. At a gathering back at the Haags' a few of my sisters very thoughtfully showed up. It was so kind of them to show their support even though I was still kind of new to the family. When it was over we returned to the city.

That autumn on a September morning, Leslie was dressing for work, I was sitting up in bed watching the morning news, when suddenly our entire building shook and the windows rattled. The TV news then switched to the downtown area just southwest of Grand Street and in shock we watched live coverage of the World Trade Center being hit by a plane. This was unbelievable. Leslie tried to get to work but the subways were down and when she finally made her way back she said that the streets were just teeming with people in tattered clothes, dusty faces, some wearing only one shoe or none at all. I had been watching the news coverage all day and the entire city was in turmoil. Somehow we still had electricity, cable, and running water but other areas that were closer to the disaster did not.

My friend Arthur Steuer lived with his girlfriend Christine along with their fifteen cats very close to the epicenter of the tragedy. They were literally just blocks away. We still had cellular service so I called begging him to come over to our place so they could at least take a shower. When they arrived, Arthur noticed the TV coverage of his neighborhood and began to cry. I gave him a set of keys to our place should they be forced to leave their apartment. A day later the wind changed and the smell of death was in the air. The trains were partially running again so I told Leslie to take the baby to work with her and I would try to get our SUV out of the parking lot and pick them up so we could escape to Ocean City.

New York City had immediately been transformed, the World Trade Center was in ruins, and the whole of downtown had become an enormous crime scene. Manhattan was in lockdown and there were police at every main intersection. I put a wet bandana around my nose and mouth and quickly began to zigzag my way over to Pier 40 on the Hudson River where we parked our car. Once there, I stopped at a folding table that had been set up by police who stood guard, and almost completely out of breath I tried to tell them that I wanted to get my vehicle, pick up my wife and child in midtown, and get out of the city. They questioned me a bit, I showed them my ID and was assigned an armed officer to escort me up the ramp to get my vehicle. On the way back down he sat in front with me, and when we reached the table again he got out and asked where I needed to go. I answered, "Fortieth and Broadway, sir." He simply said, "Get on Tenth Avenue and just go." That's exactly what I did, calling Leslie to have her meet me at the curb on the corner. I picked them both up, headed for the Lincoln Tunnel, and got out of town. I asked Leslie to call Arthur and tell him to move into our loft as soon as possible. Once in Ocean City, I suspected that some people might be trying to get through to us to make sure we were all right, so I called my mother to say that we made it to safety.

A little more than a week had gone by and we felt that we could return to the city. Manhattan was far from back to normal but the cleanup effort was well under way and power had been restored to the area around Ground Zero.

That Christmas we decided to move to the East Village, but I wanted to hold on to the place on Grand Street and turn it into a recording studio. Having a dedicated place to write and record had always been high up on my "to do" list. At the height of the very hot summer of 2002, a few of my sisters came to visit us at our new apartment on East 11th Street, and as they were touring the city there was a power brownout, of all things. I was farther downtown in Chinatown at my studio when we simply lost all power. I headed for home, hoping that the buses might still be running, which they were, but a major chunk of Manhattan was without power. My sisters somehow managed to find their way back to our place, which was a simple two bedroom apartment. We set them up in the living room with blankets and pillows so they could sleep over. In the next day or so power was eventually restored and they could return home.

We lived on East 11th Street for a while, but with Danica getting bigger, we started to feel like we needed more space. Leslie found a place in Tribeca just below Canal Street (from which the phrase was coined, the Triangle Below Canal or Tribe-ca). In fact she later told me she had noticed this particular building years before and knew that she would live there one day. Also, she had recently had an unusual encounter with a psychic who popped her head out her apartment door just as Leslie was approaching in the hall, to say that Web was there and he understood David's music now, and also told her that we would live in a place that had two interior columns.

Oddly enough, she had found the foretold apartment, columns and all. It was like we were both being led. What interested me most about Leslie's experience with the psychic was the attendance of her father and his new understanding of me and what I did for a living. It would seem that in the afterlife he came to realize that I wasn't a bum after all.

When Danica was first born we had hired a young woman named Ela who had stayed with us through all these changes, from Grand Street on. She was from Slovakia and Danica loved her; we did too. We all made the transition to the new place together. We were now living in the most expensive zip code in Manhattan. Tribeca was then home to people like Robert Di Niro and Martin Scorsese. Harvey Keitel actually lived in our building. This was impressive but we just wanted a nice home for our new family.

We continued to visit with my family as often as possible. Joan had become rather needy with her husband's passing so we spent quite a bit of time with her as well. Even though I resented Joan's leaning on us so much, I was very grateful when she agreed to look after young Danica for a few days. During Danica's stay with grandma, we managed to get out of town for a weekend in L.A. to see a new musical called *Rock of Ages*, an eighties period piece which included "Shadows of the Night" in the score. The show would eventually open on Broadway and enjoy a six-year run.

My "recreational" drug use was now at an all-time low. I hadn't seen any cocaine since Randy left town. I would occasionally smoke a bit of weed and my consumption of alcohol was now much more moderate. I was able to have a drink socially without going overboard. Finding my family, as well as becoming a father, had definitely changed me for the better. Sometime around Thanksgiving in 2004, Leslie, giving me a big hug and a kiss whispered in my ear that she was pregnant again.

CHAPTER 22

SILENT LESSONS

I
t would be a boy. Five of my seven sisters had kids. Donna had Kristofer, Denise had Heather, Amanda, and Derek, Sandy had Sarah, Toni had Brittni and Kortnee, and Dianne gave birth to her boy Rory not long after Danica was born. At the prospect of being father to a boy, naturally my mind circled back to my own childhood. There would always be shortcomings, things you later wished you had done differently. I was determined to keep those things to a minimum.

I still wanted to keep the "D. L." thing going but I didn't want a David junior or a Daniel, I was looking for something different for this boy. I came upon the name Desmond, meaning "Gracious Defender," and for a middle name chose Lucas, meaning "Light." Leslie approved and so it was.

When Leslie's water broke she went into contractions almost immediately. This kid wanted out badly. We jumped into a cab and I gave the driver our destination. For whatever reason, this crazy Russian cabdriver began to argue with me about the route that he should take. Leslie was rocking from side to side in the backseat and squeezing my arm so tightly I think that she may have been cutting off the blood supply to my brain. I never heard such screaming in my life and much of it was mine. There wasn't time for an epidural, that window had closed. Dr. Frank was literally sprinting on foot to the hospital. He barely got his gown and gloves on when the baby simply shot out of Leslie like a football, landing in the doctor's waiting hands. I watched in amazement as this baby actually became airborne for a fraction of a second before he was retrieved. He weighed in at eight pounds but seemed much bigger to us because Danica had been so tiny. Even at birth this boy displayed some real personality. I was secretly hoping that I had passed along to him some of the better parts of myself, my musicality and sense of humor.

We brought him home where he and his older sister shared a room. I was eager to bring him down to Jersey to meet my family. I was the boy that my mother had been reunited with and now there was a new boy in town.

The growing up years of our children just seemed to fly by. In contrast to my upbringing, they got to experience a fairly normal childhood. By that I mean, two parents who loved them and loved each other. I was still wrestling with how to love unconditionally and was pretty much learning on the job. My dysfunctional upbringing didn't prepare me for the hardest, most important job I would ever have. We pass on our beliefs and try to teach our offspring how to love. I never took this lightly. It's a shame there's no training for parenting, we're left to learn from experience, what's passed on through generations. Given my experiences I definitely didn't have the proper tools in my toolbox. In recent years I have met with a therapist who specializes in neuropsychology. Upon learning that I was adopted and the circumstances of my childhood home, he adamantly told me that such trauma in youth can

have a profound effect on DNA. It can take up to three generations of good parenting to eliminate such an aberration from
our genetic code. He further suggested that this can be true
whether there are family ties or not. One needs not be a blood
relative to receive transferred trauma.

I've tried my best, to be sure, but deep down I know that in
some ways I have still fallen short. Still both Leslie and I have
always sought to provide our kids with a greater sense of normalcy. Having the house on the Jersey Shore has been great
for them both. I'm sure that as they get older they will have
many fond memories. Endless summers on the beach, birthdays, holidays, had hopefully made things easier for them. We
were still seeing my new family fairly often. They were all
just a short drive from Ocean City. Even when we might be
busy with the kids, I would always speak to my mother on the
phone. She was a great comfort to me.

My eldest sister Donna's son Kristofer received a scholarship to Fairleigh Dickinson University. This was very fortunate,
as they couldn't easily afford it. But as he went off to school
something went awry. Almost right off he failed to show
up for classes and began drinking heavily, until eventually
someone found him passed out on a professor's lawn. He was
rushed to the hospital with alcohol poisoning. His scholarship
withdrawn, he was expelled. My adoptive mother had always
kept me on a very short leash, so when I went off to Peddie
I did pretty much the same kind of thing. I understood what
he might be going through although he handled it differently.
He altered his own grades, then lied to his parents about it as
well as much of the rest of the collegiate episode, and went off
to stay with my sister Kee for a while. He was in hiding and
greatly embarrassed by what he'd done. Some of my sisters
exchanged angry words with Donna and before I knew it the

entire family was being torn apart. Apparently some people said things that were just too difficult to take back. A very firm rift had taken hold between most of my sisters. Nobody was talking and I wasn't sure that whatever information I was getting, wasn't tainted with anger. This was a real problem, because not only had my newfound family quarreled so, but I had no business getting involved. I thought to intervene, put myself in the middle as a mediator of sorts, but it simply wasn't my place. The fact that my sisters shared one mother but two different fathers may have contributed to the complexity of the situation. Even with the passing of a couple of years, my sisters still hadn't come to terms with this divide. Although foreseen events would bring about a period of mutual detente.

Jeanne, our mother, was in decline. Against all sane advice she had taken out a reverse mortgage on her condo. Now nearly eighty years old, she began to experience severe physical problems. Becoming quite sedentary, she watched TV most of the day and insisted on living alone. She began to fall down in her apartment and wasn't always able to get up. This would mostly happen in the middle of the night, and somehow she would grab the phone to call my sister Toni, who lived closest, to come over and get her back into bed. This happened repeatedly until she wound up in the hospital. She really wasn't able to live alone anymore but some of my sisters seemed to be in denial, and one or two of them actually distanced themselves from the problem altogether. This created a situation that depended upon a quorum of agreement rather than a unanimous decision. Some wanted to keep her in her home because they thought that was what she wanted, but what she wanted and what was best for her were two different things. Over time things got progressively worse. She would come out of the hospital, go into rehab, return to her apartment, and the cycle would begin all over again.

Dianne found a rehabilitation facility that also had an assisted living program. She seemed to be happy there but my sisters were trying to keep her condo in place should she ever be able to come home. I contributed money to pay the taxes on the condo or something else that was needed, but that was about all that I could do. She stayed in that care facility for nearly ten months, sleeping in a hospital bed in a shared room. There was an activity center where she could spend the day watching TV or dabbling in art. She was actually a wonderful painter and truly enjoyed the process. Even though she was in a safe place and under supervision, unfortunately her health did not improve. I had been through much of this with Aunt Marie, the difference being that Marie was ambulatory until the end and was fortunate enough to actually be able to stay in her home.

It was now 2015. Danica was fourteen and Desmond ten, and we were all in Ocean City for the weekend. I was in the bedroom reading when I heard the phone ring. Leslie picked it up, I heard a very brief conversation, and then turned to see Leslie standing at the bedroom door. "That was your sister Denise," she said. "Honey, your mom just passed away . . . I'm so sorry." I sat up on the side of the bed and we hugged each other tight. I whispered, "I love you." Saying that simple phrase had never come easy to me. Throughout my life I had to teach myself how important it was. Not only important to say but equally as important to hear. I didn't cry or get angry. I just stared into space, as the whole story from the very beginning began to stream through my consciousness. Plus I was momentarily reliving my adoptive mother's death, and looking after Aunt Marie for all those years until her death.

Naturally I was upset but it was a quiet kind of upset. It was solemn, almost surreal.

I had only written one song in 2015, which was very unusual for me. It was entitled "Dancing in the Sky" and suddenly I realized why I had written it and what it was about. The maybe not so odd thing was that it was one of those rare songs that simply comes through you, like "Shadows of the Night" had done. It was as if I held the pen to the paper, blinked my eyes, and there it was. Now I knew that I had to sing that song at her funeral.

I called Scott and asked him if he had an extra microphone and a mic stand, thinking that he probably would, as he was a guitar collector like myself and an excellent musician. I couldn't even bring myself to go to my own studio to gather these things. I was virtually despondent. We arrived at the funeral home, where Denise had put together and set up a running slide show on a flat screen TV by the entrance. The photos blended so easily, moving in collage fashion, pictures from my sisters' childhood, along with shots of my mother. The blending pictures depicted years of Christmas, Halloween, and birthdays, just as one might expect to see in anyone's family history. But this was their history, not mine.

Scott walked over to me with a small bag containing exactly what I'd asked him for. I set myself up on the side of the room near the front and unpacked my twelve-string acoustic guitar. Just as when my adoptive mother passed, I could barely look at the open coffin. Apparently, I still had a problem with this sort of thing, but this wasn't about me. When it came time for me to play, the minister introduced me and without really looking at anyone, I explained that I had recently written the song but only now did I realize who it was written for. I looked straight ahead because I knew if I saw someone crying that I might not make it through the song. So I started in and managed to get through it, "So come and take my hand ... we'll let the world go by ... we'll sing 'Amazing Grace' ... and go Dancing in the Sky."

When I finished there was a moment of silence. The minister thanked me and commented on how appropriate she thought the song was. I was numb at that point but someone told me later that some people were teary-eyed. Then it was on to the burial, which was short, to the point. Afterward, everyone gathered at Denise's house where we laughed and cried, toasted our mother, and spent some time together celebrating her life. She had given so much to me. Not only had she given me life but also she restored my life and my belief in life itself. These were her silent, precious gifts, lessons that I would cherish forever.

Eventually we all kissed and hugged each other and said a sweet goodbye. A very long and lovely chapter in my life had come to a close but a new one was just beginning.

We still keep in touch either by phone or social media, and I try to get down there whenever I can. I think that some of the wounds between them have begun to heal, although Donna may still be angry, but that too will pass one day. I love all my sisters. I love them for who they are and for having accepted me so easily. Things could have certainly been very different. I will never forget my mother and the silent lessons she taught me. I'll never forget her voice, her laugh, her sharp sense of humor. Most of all I'll never forget the love that she made me feel for the first time in my life. I am eternally grateful for that.

So now, nearing the end of the story I find myself questioning how far have I actually come? What have I learned? And more importantly, what can I teach my children? I would have to answer, "Quite a bit," to all of these questions. One very important step that I took was to find peace with my adoptive mother, Ann, and appreciate what a tortured soul she was. So I have learned compassion. I have also made peace with my father, Joseph, in realizing that ignorance in others can seem like one of the hardest things to forgive. And so too I have learned forgiveness. These shadows are now mostly gone from my life. I still often find myself thinking of Aunt Marie. She taught me resilience, character, and allowed me to find an inner strength that is much more powerful than I would have ever imagined. And so I have learned to summon self-confidence and command to meet any situation whenever it should be required. The ups and downs of my career have served to make me understand that no matter who you are or where you come from, if you hold fast to your dream, that's all that matters. An interesting twist to all this is my realization that had I actually been raised by my birthmother, I might have never reached my goals. I could very likely have been living comfortably in a loving home and could have easily stayed in Jersey, eventually married, and worked at a regular job. It's an odd thing to say especially after the drama of such a glorious reunion, but I'm grateful to my birthmother for having given me up. This was a lesson in trusting in my dreams and in so doing reshaping my own shadows. As a child I fantasized that my real parents would be tremendously wealthy. My real mother was not. But in the end that didn't matter because she helped me to reshape the most daunting shadow of all and in turn gave me something greater than all the riches in the world. A peaceful and loving heart.

Just last year, I began to feel that she was still around me, and I felt that often enough to seek out a psychic just to see what might be happening. I walked into a small room and sat across from a young European woman who immediately said, "Your mother is here." I hadn't said anything about losing my mom so naturally I went along. Then she said, "Your mother wants to know if you thought she looked nice."

"What do you mean?" I questioned. "At her funeral, did you think that she looked nice . . . because she's telling me that she had picked out all her clothes ahead of time," she said. "Oh . . . oh my, I had no idea," I said. "Yes, I thought she looked very nice." All the while I was recalling that I could barely look at her during the funeral. The psychic went on, "And she wants to thank you for the thing that you made for her."

"What thing?" I wondered aloud.

"You know . . . the thing that you made," she insisted. I couldn't figure it out, what on earth she was talking about. This went back and forth for some time when suddenly it hit me. "You mean the SONG!" I said.

"Yes, yes the song, she wants to thank you for the song that you made," she said, leaning forward.

"Oh!" I said. "She's most welcome." I wanted to ask her more questions but she said that my time was up and I should visit her again. I lingered for a moment looking upward, and as hard as it had been throughout my life for me to utter these words, beneath my breath I whispered, "Mom . . . I love you!"

EPILOGUE

As the subject of adoption is central to this work, I thought that I might try to briefly address the issue directly from a layman's perspective. As depicted in the story, my adoptive parents seemed to approach adoption as a means for them to avoid the discomfort of social exclusion, not to feel left out. Outward appearances were overly important to my adoptive mother, as the story portrays. It never seemed to me as a child growing up that my parents adopted me simply because they had "so much love to give," that there was more than enough to share. Everyone around them at the time was starting a family and in that era, childless couples were often the object of scrutiny and heartless gossip by others.

What so many prospective adoptive parental candidates often fail to realize or fully understand is that simply by virtue of the physical separation of a child from its natural mother, a certain degree of trauma naturally ensues. This trauma can more than mimic but in fact reveal, at its source, the crucial and absolute importance of the genetic relationship between a child and its natural mother. As was suggested in Chapter 22, our DNA can actually be affected by trauma whether there is a blood relationship or not. This would seem to indicate that DNA is malleable and subject to interpersonal influence. Which is to imply that in my particular case, I may have inherited a shift in genetic code from my adoptive mother while still traumatized by separation from my birthmother.

This is something relatively new to scientific circles and has not been as closely examined as one might hope. Much of the research currently available has been a result of the study of Holocaust survivors. Even though that comparison may seem extreme to the subject at hand, it would seem to offer clues as to the validity of such "DNA transference" postulations. In many cases, the level of trauma can be quite severe indeed, rendering the child actually unable to feel love or a sense of belonging for much of its childhood and very possibly onward into its adult life, if left unchecked. These feelings of detachment and lack of self-worth can easily lead to a certain despondency as well as the propensity for self-sabotage, as it did for me. As science has now provided a genetic link for illnesses such as depression and alcoholism, a similar case might be made for "adoption trauma".

In my life thus far, I have met and gotten to know a number of adopted people, many of whom had personal issues not unlike the ones that I have dealt with. A few of those cases have even resulted in a tragic end. This phenomena actually seems to supersede the realm of what is considered to be normal genetics. As an adopted person who is now a parent, I can personally attest that my own son, who likely inherited my dyslexia, has shown an inordinate amount of neediness and always requires more than "normal" assurance and loving support, even though in fact he enjoyed a perfectly natural birth. This concept of transference can easily move away from conventional science into what might be termed as quantum science or even the metaphysical, in that all things are interconnected on some very real and deep level. I seem to have passed some of what I experienced as a child on to my own children, even though they were not adopted. As in the case of my adoptive parents, these things were simply unknown at the time. So unfortunately, they were ill-equipped to effectively deal with the situation. As genetic links have been scientifically established for so many maladies, I would hope for much more research on the "trauma of adoption."

I don't offer this opinion in order to dissuade anyone from the adoption process, but rather to simply point out that this innate sense of rejection that the adopted child may experience can be very real indeed. Any prospective adoptive parent should be aware that a certain understanding as well as a special skill set are required to manage and hopefully conquer these unfortunate circumstances. At the website www.cradle.org, one can find solid counseling on this subject and avail oneself of their many services. Some additional insight into the anomalies of heredity can be found at www.healthieryou.com; although this particular website focuses on alcoholism, a distinct correlation can be drawn. There is in fact much information available online by simply Googling "The heredity of separation anxiety through adoption."

I wholeheartedly believe that every child is deserving and worthy of loving parents, and any prospective parent should not be denied the love and connection that can be fully achieved once the "adoption hurdle" has been cleared. Awareness, understanding, and love are the keys to success in forging a strong relationship between any adoptee and their adoptive parents.

So if you are about to walk the path of adoption, I applaud you. I hope that you will find as much to be grateful for in your life as I have found in my own.

With that I wish you peace.

"God Goes With You"